THE MEXICAN WAR
Journal and Letters
OF RALPH W. KIRKHAM

Number Eleven
ESSAYS ON THE AMERICAN WEST
sponsored by the
Elma Dill Russell Spencer Foundation

THE MEXICAN WAR

Journal and Letters

OF RALPH W. KIRKHAM

Edited by Robert Ryal Miller

Texas A&M University Press
College Station

Frontispiece:
Ralph W. Kirkham, oil portrait bust, c. 1857
(Torres Collection)

The paper used in this book meets the minimum requirements
of the American National Standard for Permanence
of Paper for Printed Library Materials, Z39.48-1984.
Binding materials have been chosen for durability.

LIBRARY OF CONGRESS CATALOGING-IN-PUBLICATION DATA
Kirkham, Ralph W. (Ralph Wilson), 1821–
    The Mexican War Journal and letters of Ralph W.
Kirkham / edited by Robert Ryal Miller.
        p.   cm. — (Essays on the American West ;
no. 11)
    Includes bibliographical references and index.
    ISBN 0-89096-463-7 (cloth); 0-89096-537-4 (paper)
    1. Kirkham, Ralph W. (Ralph Wilson), 1821–
—Diaries.   2. Kirkham, Ralph W. (Ralph Wilson),
1821–   —Correspondence.   3. United States—
History—War with Mexico, 1845–1848—Personal nar-
natives.   4. United States—History—War with Mex-
ico, 1845–1848—Campaigns.   5. Americans—Mexico
—Diaries.   6. Americans—Mexico—Correspondence.
I. Miller, Robert Ryal.   II. Title.   III. Series.
E.411.K57   1991
973.6'28—dc20
[B]   90-41183
                                             CIP

Contents

Illustrations

Editor's Introduction

♣

RECENTLY, there has been a renewed interest in the Mexican War of 1846–48.[1] That conflict had a tremendous impact on the two belligerent nations—besides the huge financial outlay, it strained their domestic political alliances and resulted in tens of thousands of casualties. One of the major effects of the war was the peace treaty's territorial adjustment that transferred to the United States more than half a million square miles, an area larger than Spain, France, and Italy combined. For the United States, the acquisition of vast new lands provided room for expansion and ports on the Pacific, but the newly acquired lands upset the balance of free and slave states, intensifying sectionalism, which helped to bring on the American Civil War. For Mexicans, the war was an economic and psychological disaster. The disgrace of losing virtually all of the battles, having their capital and other cities occupied by the enemy, and being forced to surrender half their national territory (counting Texas), shattered national honor and engendered a deep-seated Yankeephobia. Mexicans continue to lament the consequences of that war.

Forty years ago, when I studied history at Mexico's Universidad Nacional Autónoma, Professor Pablo Martínez del Río organized field trips for his students to visit nearby battle sites of the U.S.-Mexican War. His lectures and those excursions kindled my interest in U.S.-Mexican relations and led to many subsequent visits to Mexico. But while climbing around the fortresses of Churubusco and Chapultepec, little did I realize then that I would have a career of teaching Mexican history at American universities, and that one day I would discover an original manuscript journal written by a Yankee officer who fought at those memorable battlegrounds.

A number of American officers and soldiers kept diaries or journals during the Mexican War. Of the surviving accounts, some are now located in archives and libraries; others have been published as books or articles in historical quarterlies; and perhaps a few are in family trunks or attics. Most of the printed accounts described events during the campaigns of Generals Zachary Taylor and Stephen Kearny in Mexico's northern states and territories, but operations in the southern theater of war were not as well covered. Just a few eyewitnesses chronicled General Winfield Scott's amphibious landing near Veracruz and his subsequent battles leading to the takeover of Mexico City, and only three of the previously published accounts spanned the important nine months' military occupation of Mexico's capital.[2] Thus the recently discovered journal kept by Lieutenant Ralph Kirkham during the last fifteen months of the American military presence in the heartland of Mexico is a welcome and important addition to the Mexican War literature. Kirkham's lively and compelling account has descriptive and literary merits, but it is chiefly valuable as a first-person memoir and primary historical source. Furthermore, the lieutenant's observations are astute and accurate.

Ralph Wilson Kirkham was from New England, where his family roots extended back to 1640. His great-great-grandfather, Henry Kirkham, fought in the French and Indian War, and his grandfather, John Kirkham, served in the American Revolution, during which he was wounded at the Battle of Monmouth. Lieutenant Kirkham's father was assessor, collector, and a selectman of Springfield, Massachusetts, a textile center and site of an important armory one hundred miles west of Boston.[3] Springfield had a population of about 6,200 people in 1821, when Ralph, the second of five children born to John Butler Kirkham and Betsy Wilson Kirkham, was born there.[4] His early years were typical of a middle-class boy's life at that period — he went to public school, tramped in the woods, fished in the Connecticut River, and played games in the winter snow. When he was sixteen, he went to Geneva, New York, where he studied at the Lyceum (which later became Hobart College) for two years. Then he taught school for one year at Granville, New York, before beginning his true vocation.[5]

In February, 1838, Kirkham received a printed notice from the secretary of war appointing him a cadet at the U.S. Military Academy, effective June 30 of that year. He had been nominated by Congressman William B. Calhoun. For the next four years he studied, drilled, and lived at West Point, New York. He liked the beautiful setting on the Hudson River, the physical contact games, horseback riding, swimming, and escapades with fellow cadets at the nearby tavern operated by Benny Havens and his wife. His classes included mathematics, civil

U.S. Military Academy cadet uniforms, 1840 (U.S. Military Academy Library)

and military engineering, chemistry, geography, history, philosophy, French, and drawing.[6] During those cadet years, Kirkham kept a notebook in which he listed alphabetically the members of his class, their home states, and a brief note about their careers at the academy and later. Of the 114 young men who entered in 1838, plus three who were turned back from earlier classes, only 56 successfully completed the four years. Two cadets died during those years, 21 resigned, 7 were dismissed, and 31, those who failed their examinations, were found to be "deficient."[7]

Upon graduation in 1842, Ralph Kirkham was commissioned as a second lieutenant in the infantry branch of the United States Army. Following a leave of absence, during which he visited his family in Springfield, Massachusetts, he reported for duty at Fort Niagara, New York. Like other graduates of the academy, Kirkham expected to stay in the army at least four years, because Congress had stipulated such a requirement in 1838.[8] A second lieutenant's pay was then twenty-five dollars a month plus rations. Prospects for promotion, which was by seniority within each regiment, were slim because the army was barely growing and because there was no retirement system, which induced many officers to remain on active duty until an advanced age.

After six months of duty at Fort Niagara, Lieutenant Kirkham was reassigned to the Indian Territory of Oklahoma, more than a thousand miles away. He traveled most of the way by riverboat — down the Ohio to its junction with the Mississippi, then south on that river to Fort Smith, Arkansas, where he took a steamboat up the Arkansas River to Fort Gibson. During the next four years he served with the Sixth Infantry Regiment at two frontier posts in the Cherokee Nation: Fort Gibson, near the junction of the Arkansas River and the Neosho (or Grand) River; and at Fort Towson, one hundred and twenty miles south, near the confluence of the Red and Kiamichi rivers. These western forts were established in the 1820s to protect the routes of travel, and to implement the government's Indian removal policy.[9]

Romance bloomed for Lieutenant Kirkham at Fort Gibson in 1846. On June 1 of that year he met Miss Catherine E. Mix, two years younger than himself, who had come to the post to visit her Aunt Julia, wife of the post commander, Colonel Gustavus Loomis.[10] For Ralph and Catherine, it was love at first sight; they were engaged in mid-July, and married in the post chapel on October 20. Born in Washington, D.C., Catherine Mix had been raised in New Orleans, Louisiana, where she had a father and six brothers.[11] After their marriage, Ralph and Kate Kirkham enjoyed five months of bliss, living in a small cottage at Fort Gibson. They had a servant named "Aunt Hetty," two dogs, some cats, chickens, and a garden.[12] But the war

Catherine Mix Kirkham, oil portrait bust, c. 1857 (Torres Collection)

with Mexico, which began in 1846, separated the Kirkhams when he was ordered to the battlefront.

Two decades of deteriorating relations between the two countries led to the Mexican War. Beginning in the 1820s, Mexican leaders were apprehensive about the expansionist tendencies of the United States, which had recently acquired the Louisiana Territory and Florida, and they worried about the growing number of American trappers, traders, explorers, and settlers who moved into their northern provinces.

Some of those Yankees were stimulated by a sentiment called Manifest Destiny—the belief that divine providence had given the United States a moral mission to occupy and develop western lands. Perhaps this same spirit, as well as their own imperial ambitions, motivated three American presidents to send agents to Mexico offering to purchase California, New Mexico, or Texas—proposals that were offensive to Mexican officials.[13]

Two of the American schemes to purchase Mexican territory were tied to the problem of Mexico's debts and its nearly bankrupt condition. In 1842 President John Tyler instructed the American minister to try to acquire California in exchange for the cancellation of Mexico's debts to the United States. Three years later President James Polk dispatched a special envoy to Mexico empowered to offer $5 million for the western half of New Mexico and $25 million for California, and to propose the assumption of a $2-million unpaid debt to the United States in exchange for Mexican recognition of the Rio Grande as the boundary between the two nations. This delinquent debt involved claims for repudiated bonds, revoked concessions, and damages to American property that had occurred during civil wars in Mexico. Although Mexico had signed a convention in 1843 to pay the debt, it suspended payments the following year.[14]

Texas and its boundary were central issues in the controversy between the United States and Mexico. In 1836, after the Texans won their war of independence with Mexico, they established an independent republic, which Mexico refused to recognize. Furthermore, the new nation declared its southwestern boundary to be the Rio Grande (Río Bravo y Grande del Norte) from its mouth to its source, thereby shifting the line many miles southwest of the Nueces River, the traditional boundary. This exaggerated claim tripled the size of the old Spanish and Mexican Texas, and it put the eastern half of New Mexico, including Albuquerque and Santa Fe, into the Lone Star Republic. Several times during the nine years of Texas independence, emissaries from that republic asked for annexation to the United States, a request that provoked heated debate in Washington and elsewhere. Northern antislavery forces did not want to add another slave state to the Union, but southern planters favored the move, as did northern expansionists. Meanwhile, Mexican officials accused the United States of complicity with Texas in its independence war and declared that annexation "would mean war with Mexico."[15]

American moves to acquire Texas culminated in 1845. At the end of February, just before the inauguration of President Polk, who had campaigned for the acquisition of Texas and Oregon, a joint congressional resolution invited Texas to join the Union, if Texans themselves ratified the agreement. A week later the Mexican minister in Washington, claiming that the resolution was "an act of aggression," broke off diplomatic relations and returned home. In July, a popular convention in Texas voted to join the Union, and five months later the American Congress declared Texas the twenty-eighth state. Meanwhile, as soon as Texas agreed to annexation, Polk sent a naval squadron to the Gulf Coast and an occupation army to Texas to protect the new American state against a threatened Mexican attack. A few of Polk's contemporaries and several historians have asserted that the president sent the large military force to the Texas frontier hoping to provoke an attack by Mexico, after which the United States would retaliate by seizing California and other Mexican territory. Certainly, Polk wanted California, by peaceful acquisition if possible.[16]

Brigadier General Zachary Taylor headed the American troops that established a camp, at the end of July, 1845, on the west bank of the Nueces River near its mouth at Corpus Christi, Texas. Additional soldiers arrived during the following months; by October the force numbered thirty-nine hundred men, which was almost half of the United States Army. Early in 1846, when Polk learned that Mexican officials had refused to receive John Slidell, his special emissary sent to settle the Texas annexation and boundary questions, he ordered Taylor to advance to the left bank of the Rio Grande, where he was to take up a defensive position.[17] The Rio Grande boundary claimed by Texas was also sustained by the United States, but Mexico claimed that the land between the Nueces and the Rio Grande was its territory.

At the end of March, 1846, Taylor established a forward base about twenty-five miles upriver from the mouth of the Rio Grande and opposite the Mexican town of Matamoros. There, American soldiers constructed a five-sided fortress with earthen walls nine feet high and fifteen feet thick. Facing them across the river was a Mexican army garrison that was reinforced in April by three thousand additional soldiers. The Mexican commander ordered the Americans to decamp and retreat to the other side of the Nueces River, but Taylor replied that his instructions did not permit a withdrawal. After a Mexican cavalry column of sixteen-hundred men crossed the river with orders to cut the

American supply line, there was an inevitable clash. Hostilities began on April 25, 1846, when an American scouting party was ambushed by a Mexican unit in the disputed territory on the left bank. In that engagement, eleven Yankees were killed, six wounded, and sixty-three taken prisoner.[18]

When President Polk was notified about the bloodshed on the Rio Grande, he incorporated this fateful news into a special message he had already prepared for Congress, asking for a declaration of war. Announcing news of the armed clash, he told the legislators, "Mexico has passed the boundary of the United States, has invaded our territory and shed American blood upon the American soil. . . . A war exists, and notwithstanding all our efforts to avoid it, exists by the act of Mexico herself. . . ." Influenced by these assertions, and other arguments such as that regarding the unpaid claims, the overwhelming majority of legislators voted, on May 13, to declare a war on Mexico. The vote was 174 to 14 in the House, and 40 to 2 in the Senate. Mexico's Congress delayed its declaration of war to July 2.[19]

Public opinion about the Mexican War was sharply divided in the United States. In Congress the great majority of legislators favored the war and voted for funds to pursue it, but a vociferous minority, including Daniel Webster, John Quincy Adams, and Abraham Lincoln opposed it. Enthusiastic public gatherings in major cities generated support for the war and stimulated enlistment of volunteers, especially in the Mississippi Valley, where thousands of men enlisted for service in Mexico. Yet there was enough dissent to classify this as an "unpopular war." In addition to the partisan opposition of the Whigs, who faulted the Democrats and their president, some Americans considered the war to be unjustified aggression against a weak neighbor; abolitionists thought that it was a conspiracy of slaveholders to extend their territory; and still others blamed New England merchants and shippers who coveted Pacific Coast ports.[20]

When the war began, U.S. strategy, outlined in cabinet meetings and at military headquarters in Washington, called for naval units to blockade Mexico's principal ports in the Gulf and on the Pacific, while land forces would seize territory west and south of Texas. Eventually, five separate American armies invaded Mexico, where they participated in more than fifty campaigns and engagements. General Zachary Taylor's Army of Occupation crossed the Rio Grande at Matamoros and eventually captured Monterrey and other northern cities.

General John Wool's Central Division moved southwest from San Antonio to Saltillo for a timely linkup with Taylor. General Stephen Kearny marched his men from Fort Leavenworth to Santa Fe, New Mexico, where they raised the American flag. Then Kearny took part of his forces to occupy California, which had been partially subdued by American naval and marine units, aided by mounted Yankee riflemen under Major John Frémont. One column of Kearny's army, under Colonel Alexander Doniphan, marched south from New Mexico to Chihuahua and Saltillo. Finally, a large amphibious force under General Winfield Scott landed on the Gulf Coast near Veracruz and followed in Hernán Cortés's footsteps to conquer Mexico City.[21]

Lieutenant Ralph Kirkham joined Scott's forces about a month after the Americans had landed near Veracruz. Ordered to join the Sixth Infantry headquarters, then based in Perote, Mexico, Kirkham left Fort Gibson at the end of March, 1847. His wife Kate accompanied him to New Orleans, where she would spend the first part of the war years, and where he would board a ship for Veracruz and duty in the combat zone. Kirkham, who played the flute, also escorted to Mexico the band of the Sixth Infantry. His journal entries began on March 27, 1847, when he boarded a steamboat at Fort Gibson bound for New Orleans.

In his journal and letters to his wife Kirkham gave vivid details of his wartime service in Mexico. His position as adjutant general of the Sixth Infantry Regiment and assistant adjutant general of the second brigade of Major General William Worth's First Division gave him an opportunity to observe different military outfits and operations. Because he was required to keep records of his regiment and to serve as liaison between his unit and others, he always had access to paper and ink, a scarce commodity on campaigns. Kirkham portrayed scenery and events while en route to Mexico's capital, especially in the city of Puebla, where Scott's army remained for three months. Later he graphically described six major battles on the outskirts of Mexico City. During these engagements he saw many of his classmates and comrades wounded or killed. As a result of his gallantry in Mexico, Kirkham received a brevet promotion (an honorary rank higher than his permanent pay grade) to first lieutenant and later to captain.

After the American takeover of Mexico City in mid-September, 1847, and during the subsequent nine months of peace negotiations, Kirk-

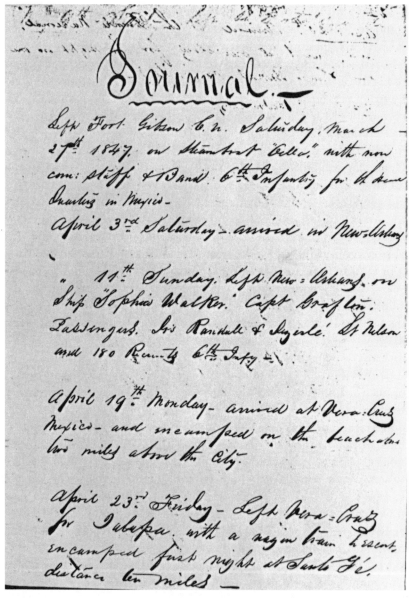

First page of Kirkham's journal (Torres Collection)

ham continued to write about the U.S. military occupation of the heartland of Mexico and about his own activities there. His comments show
that there was considerable collaboration between Mexican civilians
and American military personnel. In the Mexican capital and in Toluca, where he was based for two months, he was treated kindly by
Mexicans, who entertained him and other officers in their homes and
haciendas.

Although Kirkham was a professional soldier, his observations were
not limited to military matters. Among other highlights, he described
a Mexican bullfight, the effects of an earthquake, the funeral of a young
Mexican girl, a visit to a Mexican theater, and a Lenten carnival which
featured a colorful public procession with musical groups and masked
dancers. In one long letter he recalled his trek, along with five other
officers, to the summit of the volcano Popocatepetl, which rises to 17,887
feet above sea level. This is the first known ascent by any American
to the summit and crater of that perpetually snow-peaked mountain,
which is visible from the Mexican capital.

Kirkham also commented about what he saw on visits to several
institutions in Mexico City. He described some of the paintings and
sculpture at the Academia Nacional de Bellas Artes, artifacts from
Aztec and other Indian cultures on display at the Museo Nacional,
and the artwork and architecture of the Hospital de Jesús, founded
three centuries earlier by Hernán Cortés. He also noted the profu-
sion of flowering plants such as dahlias and passion flowers, and of
fruit trees, including pomegranates, quinces, figs, olives, and citrus.
In the countryside he jotted down the names of crops he saw growing
in the fields.

Of special interest are Kirkham's descriptions of Mexican residences.
For two months he was billeted in a private home in Toluca, about
forty-five miles southwest of Mexico City, where he ate with the family. Meals began in the morning with hot chocolate; the midday dinner consisted of eight to ten courses; chocolate or coffee and bread
were available at five each afternoon; and a substantial supper was
served at about seven in the evening. Among the regional foods mentioned, he liked green pea pie and pumpkin preserves. Later, when
quartered in the Mexico City home of a Mexican colonel, Kirkham
described the palatial residence, which featured a large central patio
with a myriad of flowers and an aviary containing more than one hundred colorful songbirds. He also reflected on a Christmas Eve party

which he attended in a private home in the capital where the owners had an entire room fixed up as a Nativity scene.

Kirkham's religious spirit is evident in many of his journal entries. A devout Episcopalian, he often jotted down prayers — sometimes as thanks for having survived a battle, and sometimes asking divine protection for his wife. He also made negative comments about Roman Catholic priests and practices in Mexico. Several times Kirkham mentioned Protestant religious services conducted by the Rev. John Mc-Carty, the only commissioned American army chaplain who served in Mexico. These devotional services always made the young lieutenant think of his wife and family in the United States, and he longed to return home. Finally, in midsummer of 1848, after witnessing the replacement of the American by the Mexican flag over the Palacio Nacional of Mexico, Kirkham and his unit headed back to Veracruz, where they boarded ship for home.

Over the years, the letters Lieutenant Kirkham sent to his wife from Mexico and his journal kept in that country have remained with his family, who considered them precious souvenirs. Heretofore, they have never been seen by outsiders. Two of Kirkham's great-granddaughters, Sarah J. Torres and Arian Gedman, have inherited and carefully preserved these items, along with his silver spurs, golden epaulettes, and other family mementos. I am indebted to them for making these written items and the portraits of Kirkham and his wife available for publication. They also were extremely helpful in identifying relatives mentioned in the journal and in providing genealogical data.

Information about American arms and military organization during the Mexican War came from several sources. Richard J. Sommers, archivist-historian at the U.S. Military History Institute, Carlisle Barracks, Pennsylvania, answered specific questions and provided additional information that aided the editing process. Two friends, George Rascoe and Colonel James Harvey Short, both of whom attended the Military Academy at West Point, kindly made their extensive military libraries available to me. Finally, I must thank the staff of the Bancroft Library at the University of California, Berkeley, for providing study space and for locating pertinent books and relevant documents.

In editing Kirkham's journal and letters, very few changes were made. Dates of journal entries were standardized for uniformity, several Mexican placenames were given their modern spellings, punctuation marks were occasionally inserted, and some extremely long passages were broken into paragraphs. Brackets or footnotes were used to correct errors in the text, to provide further information about a subject mentioned, and to identify the more than one hundred and thirty persons mentioned—army officers, Mexican and American civilians, and relatives. In a few cases where the journal and letters repeated the same story, one account was eliminated. In comparing the text of the journal and the letters, it is interesting to note what information the lieutenant chose to tell his wife and what he reserved for his private notebook. As the reader will soon discover, Lieutenant Kirkham wrote clear, forceful prose that is as readable today as when he penned it more than a hundred and forty years ago.

ROBERT RYAL MILLER
Berkeley, California

THE MEXICAN WAR
Journal and Letters
OF RALPH W. KIRKHAM

CHAPTER ONE

New Orleans to Puebla

JOURNAL, March 27, 1847. Aboard Steamboat *Oilla.*

Left Fort Gibson, C.N. [Cherokee Nation], Saturday, [March 27] on Steamboat *Oilla* with non-com[missioned] staff & band, 6th Infantry, for the [regimental] headquarters in Mexico.

JOURNAL, April 3, 1847. New Orleans.

Arrived in New Orleans.

JOURNAL, April 11, 1847. Aboard ship *Sophia Walker.*

Left New Orleans on ship *Sophia Walker,* Captain Grafton. Passengers: Drs. Randall and Deyerle, Lt. Nelson, and 180 recruits, 6th Infantry.[1]

LETTER, April 18, 1847. Aboard *Sophia Walker* off Veracruz.

My Dear Wife:

God Bless you my dear little Kate. To think after having been so happy together for the past six months we are now separated. Not a day passes that I do not dwell on the quiet happiness of our Fort Gibson cottage. I used to think I had a stout heart and could brave the ups and downs of the world with fortitude, but I give up now. Restore me to the quiet and contented home and all my ambition is gone. Today is Sunday, but, oh how differently we are spending it from what we used to do. I have been sitting on the deck humming over the hymns we used to sing together, but I gave it up, sad at heart.

I wonder if you are rid of your cold. Has Dr. McCormick been to see you?[2] I have been so seasick until today that I have been unable to leave my stateroom or eat anything. I am getting bravely over it now. You need have no fears about me, for as soon as I get ashore I shall be myself again. You know I have a strong constitution. Joseph [a servant brought from New Orleans] is perfectly at home on the ship, not at all seasick; he has eaten his rations ever since we started.[3]

How long do you think you will stay in New Orleans? I am afraid to have you there during the summer, as I think the air of the country will be better for you. I hope you will go to [your sister Sophie's home in] Alton [Illinois].

We are about eighty miles from Veracruz. As soon as I know, after my arrival there, when we go into the interior, I will write you.

JOURNAL, April 19, 1847. Veracruz.

Arrived at Veracruz, Mexico, and encamped on the beach about two miles above the city.

LETTER, April 19, 1847. Veracruz.

My Dear Wife:

Here we are at last. I have been running around the city nearly all day merely to gratify my curiosity for we shall be detained here probably two or three days and much to my regret. We have not disembarked our traps [baggage] and are now lying between the castle and the town.[4] Tomorrow I intend visiting the former. The town is a miserable place, and since our shots [during the land and sea bombardment from March 22 to 26] have demolished a great many of the houses and ruined the walls to a great many more, it looks really pitiful. The city is built entirely of brick and stone. There is hardly a tree or any shrubbery in sight of it. The walls surrounding the city ought to have protected it if the [Mexican] troops had had any skill; with five thousand men we could have held it against ten times the number. Our balls seem to have penetrated nearly every house in town, completely demolishing many.

We got the news this evening, just before I left the town, by Kendall's Express, which is ahead of the government one, that General Scott met [Mexican General] Santa Anna at the pass of Cerro Gordo [about sixty miles inland from Veracruz], and after a most desperate conflict on both sides, succeeded in obtaining a victory.[5] Scott had about 8,000 troops; Santa Anna had 15,000 [actually, about 9,000]. Our loss, killed and wounded, is about 1,000; the Mexican loss is unknown, but far greater than ours, and we have 6,000 prisoners.[6] I do

Major General Winfield Scott (Vincente Riva Palacio, ed., *México através de los siglos,* 5 vols. [Mexico City, 1887–89], 4:681)

not know how the 6th Regiment behaved. Oh, I wish I had been there! Tomorrow we shall get particulars, but I want to send this by the *Columbia* which sails at daybreak. Many think that this will be the last battle and that we are going to camp in the upper country.

Now do not worry the least about me. I never was in better health and spirits in my life. Take good care of yourself. Your letters will produce more impression than the Mexicans, and when I return from the war, what a good time we will have! God bless you. Remember our motto, "Hope on; hope ever." Your ever affectionate husband.

LETTER, April 22, 1847. Veracruz.

My Dear Little Kate:

I have not yet been able to get away from this place. We are camped on the shore about two miles from the city. We hope to get transportation to leave in the morning, and would have gotten off before, but as my men are only armed with their musical instruments, I did not like to start alone. There is not the least danger with even a small armed detachment, but hardly a day passes without someone being wounded or killed traveling alone. Yesterday, almost within sight of our camp, they [Mexican guerrillas] killed a teamster. His wagon had broken down and he was left behind the train. He was brought into camp last night with three bullets through him. We will have upwards of 200 in our party. The rascals will not presume to even show themselves to us.

I wrote you the day we landed. I gave you the rumors of General Scott's battle [at Cerro Gordo on April 17–18]. You have learned before this reaches you that the reports are somewhat exaggerated. I lost a classmate in the fight, Lieutenant Dana. He was mortally wounded and is probably now dead.[7] I was very intimate with him at West Point, and we were confirmed together [in the Episcopal church].

Joseph [my servant] is getting along as usual. He seems to enjoy the change.

Well, I will say goodbye. Please write often even if you do not say more than a dozen words. Address: [c/o] 6th U.S. Infantry, General Scott's Army, Mexico. Please number all your letters to me.

Your ever affectionate husband.

JOURNAL, April 23, 1847. Santa Fé.

Left Veracruz for Jalapa with a wagon train to escort. Encamped first night at Santa Fé, distance ten miles.

JOURNAL, April 25, 1847. Hacienda [Manga de Clavo].

Arrived at the Puente Nacional [National Bridge], and quartered ourselves for the night in one of Santa Anna's haciendas.

LETTER, April 26, 1847. National Bridge, en route to Jalapa.

My Dear Little Wife:

Here we are at one of Santa Anna's country residences.[8] It is a beautiful place. We got in early in the evening, have had our dinner and a delightful bath in the river [Río Antigua]. We might have marched some eight or ten miles farther on, but the quarters were so inviting we concluded to stay here. The house is really splendid, although the furniture is all or nearly all gone, just the bare white walls, with the exception of a few chairs, tables, etc. It seems strange to me to be here, and more strange still to see upwards of two hundred soldiers quartered in this house.

While I am writing, our band is playing our national airs in honor of some news we have just got from Jalapa. I do not know whether to credit it all or not. It amounts to this: General Worth with his command, and my [6th] regiment is with him, have taken Perote, and without firing a shot. They captured 200 cannon. They also report that General Taylor has taken San Luis Potosí.[9] [The last rumor was false.] I wish I was up with my regiment, but the [American military] governor of Veracruz has put under our charge a train of forty wagons to escort, and we cannot march more than fifteen miles a day on account of the mules, which are Mexican and the meanest little animals I have ever seen. We will get there in two days more, I think.

I have wished all along the road that you were with me for I have seen so many beautiful flowers, fruits, and birds, all new to me, and here the view is really grand. The bridge across the river is a fine piece of art, flanked with high bluffs upon which are built some small forts for the defense of the bridge, and it is a wonder to me that we were

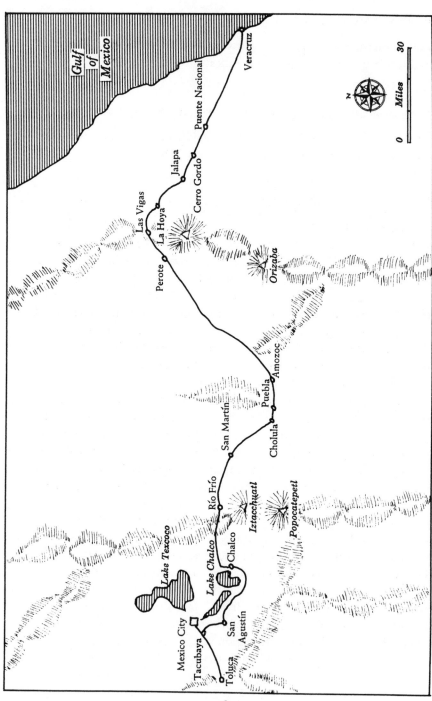

Kirkham's Route in Mexico (map by Robert R. Miller)

Gulf
of
Mexico

Veracruz

Puente Nacional

Jalapa

Cerro Gordo

Las Vigas
La Hoya

Perote

Orizaba

Amozoc

Puebla

San Martín

Cholula

Río Frío

Iztacchuatl

Popocatepetl

Lake Texcoco

Lake Chalco

Chalco

Mexico City

Tacubaya

San Agustín

Toluca

Miles

0   30

8

General Antonio López de Santa Anna (Lucas Alamán, *Historia de Méjico,*
5 vols. [Mexico City, 1849–52], 5:687)

able to get past here. If the Mexicans had any bravery, we certainly
should have had to fight pretty hard for it. They are principally shooting down stragglers on the road. We picked up two yesterday who
were murdered the day before. We buried them beside the road. The
men seem to have little judgment about leaving the main body, but
go just where their inclination leads them.

You must have no fears about me for we have already got into the
Upper Country and I expect to enjoy better health this summer than

I have since I left the North. At Jalapa they are eating ice cream, and at Perote, where my regiment is, it is so cold that they have to sleep under three blankets. This [last] is just what suits me. I have got my bed intact, just as it was packed when I left Fort Gibson, mattress and all. Capital, is it not?

This will go by express to Veracruz tomorrow. Goodnight.

Your ever affectionate husband.

Journal, April 28, 1847. Jalapa.

Arrived at Jalapa. Found here General Scott with General Twigg's and Quitman's brigades, General Worth with his division having gone on to Perote.[10]

Letter, April 29, 1847. Jalapa.

My dear wife:

I have only time to say that I am getting along capitally. The air and water here are the purest in the world. I arrived here last night and leave this evening or tomorrow morning. It seems that everybody is here, more generals and officers than I have ever met before. I have found several of my [West Point] classmates. Yesterday we stopped some eight or ten miles back of the road at another of Santa Anna's haciendas, and it is really a most beautiful place.[11] A great deal of money has been expended on it. Everything in the house indicates luxury and splendor, and in the city [of Jalapa], in the way of sup- plying the table, there is everything to be had. Tomorrow or next day I hope to be with my own regiment, and soon afterwards I shall know whether I go to my company or retain my adjutancy. I do not care much which.

This morning I went to the cathedral and heard mass. I believe I should become a strict Catholic should I live in a Catholic country, for I do like an everyday religion. I wish you could have been with me this morning and heard the solemn tones of the organ and seen the hundreds [of people] kneeling on the stone floor. I came near going with the rest, but made several good resolutions which I hope I shall keep.

It is a month today since we left Fort Gibson and three weeks since we parted. I hardly know how to direct this letter, to Alton [Illinois] or New Orleans, but I think you will get it anyhow.

I wrote in my next to last letter that Lieutenant Dana was killed. It was a false report. I saw him this morning. He was severely wounded but will recover. Goodbye.

May God bless you, is the prayer of your affectionate husband.

JOURNAL, April 30, 1847. Las Vigas.

Left Jalapa; traveled some seven or eight miles and encamped. The next day we stopped at Las Vigas.

JOURNAL, May 2, 1847. Perote.

Arrived at Perote and reported to Colonel Clarke, 6th Infantry, whom we found in command of the 2nd brigade of General Worth's [first] division. The brigade is composed of the 5th, 6th, and 8th Regiments of Infantry.[12]

JOURNAL, May 3, 1847. Castle of Perote.

Was informed by Colonel Clarke that he wished me to continue [as] adjutant of my regiment. He also appointed me the acting assistant adjutant general of his brigade. I removed today from the town to the Castle of Perote, which lies about half a mile out in the plain.[13]

LETTER, May 4, 1847. Castle of Perote.

My Dear Kate:

I know you have written me several times, but as I have been traveling farther from you, I have not received your letters. I arrived at the town of Perote on the 2nd. I reported to Colonel Clarke, was received with every cordiality, and when I resigned my adjutancy, he declined accepting it, and further, made me his adjutant general to the 2nd brigade of General Worth's division, which he commands. I have had hardly a moment to myself since I arrived, for besides my regimental duties I have to make details from and publish orders to the three

U.S. Army at Perote fortress (J. Jacob Oswandel, *Notes of the Mexican War* [Philadelphia, 1885], p. 179)

regiments: the 5th, 6th, and 8th Infantry, which compose Colonel Clarke's brigade.

I have no trouble about messing, Colonel Clarke having invited me to join his mess. There are four of us: Colonel Clarke; Mr. Mc-Carty, the chaplain of our brigade; Lieutenant Burwell, Colonel Clarke's aide-de-camp; and myself. I am delighted to get with my regiment once more. I met many old friends and many inquired for you. Captain Cady and Lieutenant Fitzgerald have called to see me.[14]

I am living in the castle. You cannot imagine the strangeness of this place. We have not in the United States any fortifications that will compare with it in expense and skill with which it is constructed. It cost five million, and is a perfect fortification.[15] It is very cold here. I am writing with my overcoat on and sleeping at night under all the blankets I can get. We are so high up [7,900 feet] that the clouds rest on the plain on which the castle is built. As we are in the midst of clouds half of the day, we are nearly wet through by the moisture of the atmosphere, and yet we are so near the tropical country that a few hours' ride will bring one to the land of oranges, pineapples, and bananas.

We have orders to march in the morning but probably will not get off until next day. General Worth's division takes the lead, and the 6th Regiment goes ahead. So if there is any fighting, we shall be near enough to see it, at least I hope so. But there is to be no fighting at Puebla, the next place of importance. We expect no opposition; in fact we hear that the inhabitants have had the barracks put in order to receive us. The Mexicans have resolved on a guerrilla mode of warfare and will not again meet a large body of troops. They intend to cut off small parties wherever they find an opportunity. They will not catch me, for I move with three regiments.

I am so glad that we have a chaplain, and he is an Episcopalian and an excellent man. How many blessings I enjoy—friends, health, happiness and prosperity in every respect, and yet how unworthy I am!

If we leave tomorrow I do not know when I shall hear from you. Still our motto is "Hope on; hope ever." It is not more than 65 or 70 miles to Puebla, and there we will be in a city of 80,000 inhabitants and the finest climate in the world.

Everybody is delighted with my band. It is said by all who have heard it to be the finest in the army. It is playing this evening for General Worth. Last evening we had it here at the castle.

I dined with General Worth the day I arrived. He is a splendid soldier and worthy of the troops he commands.

I have lost poor Joseph. On the road from Jalapa I met his stepfather, who is a sergeant in the 2nd Dragoons. He was very anxious to get him back, so I let him go. I think it is better, for he was of little use to me in the field. I wish I had John, but I shall get along well enough.

I have found here in my quarters a great many letters signed by Santa Anna. I will send one to you in this letter, also one of Guadalupe Victoria, and one of General Almonte. They will be something of a curiosity.[16]

When shall we meet again, God only knows. Before not a great while, I hope. Good Night.

Ever your affectionate husband.

LETTER, May 8, 1847. Castle of Perote.

My Dearest Kate:

We have orders to march in the morning at 7 o'clock. So I have sat down this evening after having been very busy in getting off two

Brigadier General William J. Worth (Anderson, *An Artillery Officer in the Mexican War,* p. 110)

regiments of our brigade. The 6th left this morning and presented a fine appearance with their colors flying and the band playing. The 5th left at two in the afternoon, and the 8th brings up the rear in the morning. I am so glad that I am with the advance troops. General Twiggs's division was in the vanguard at the battle of Cerro Gordo, but General Worth's division has the lead now and we keep it until we get to Puebla. I will send you a concise notice of the distance to the city. You see we make short marches. It takes five days to go.

I will be glad to leave this place, and yet there are a great many attractions in the neighborhood. But I have been so busy that I have had no leisure. My greatest happiness is to catch a momentary glance of your miniature; it is precious to me indeed. I should be unhappy should I lose it. I have to get up at reveille, and it is a little different from our Fort Gibson custom. However, it is better for me. Several of my classmates, whom I have not met since we graduated in 1842, have told me that I have not changed in appearance at all.

You know I threatened when I got among the Mexican girls to play the gallant. I have not found time yet, and besides I have only seen one girl here who had even a pretty face. I saw her at mass in the cathedral in Jalapa. I judged she was thinking more of an officer beside her than she was of her prayer book, or her beads which she was counting. But she was pretty! Such beautiful large, dark eyes and such a graceful figure, and she wore her rebozo [shawl] so coquettishly. I believe I should have followed her, but a very sour, cross-grained duenna [*dueña*] who was with her made me change my mind. If you will write me that you are at all jealous, I will call and see her when I return to Jalapa. But such eyes! And they nearly resembled those of my own dear Katie.

I do not know when I shall hear from you. The mail came today, but no letters for me. I think there is an express going to leave this evening so I must send this to the office. Goodbye for today.

Your truly affectionate husband.

JOURNAL, May 9, 1847. San Antonio.

Left La Fortaleza de Perote and advanced some eight miles and encamped at San Antonio. It was so cold this night that ice formed in the open air.

JOURNAL, May 12, 1847. El Pinal.

The whole of General Worth's division encamped at El Pinal. Our advance guards were here fired upon by a body of Mexican lancers. The whole army was under arms from 1 o'clock until reveille.[17]

JOURNAL, May 13, 1847. Amozoc.

Arrived at Amozoque [Amozoc] and took quarters in some stable yards in town.

JOURNAL, May 14, 1847. Amozoc.

This morning Santa Anna came out from Puebla with about 3,000 cavalry. He passed around the town within a mile or two, as though his intention was to get in our rear. We left the town and went out to meet him, planted our batteries and opened fire. But the enemy soon showed signs of retreat, and in one hour not a Mexican was to be seen. As we have but few dragoons, we did not pursue them.[18]

CHAPTER TWO

In the City of Puebla

JOURNAL, May 15, 1847. Puebla.

Marched into the city of Puebla, or La Puebla de los Angeles, as the Mexicans call it. A deputation had been sent out from the city the night before and invited General Worth to the city. No resistance was to be made. The city is completely under cover of two forts which occupy the heights just out of the city: Forts Loreto & Guadalupe. The 5th Infantry was detached to garrison these forts, Santa Anna having "vamoosed" with his army and taken the road to the city of Mexico. We understand that he is at San Martín [Texmelucan] fortifying himself.

LETTER, May 19, 1847. Puebla.

Dear Katie:

I wrote you a few days ago, but I have learned that the Mexicans have murdered two of our express [couriers] and got the mails within the past week. So I will write again even if this does not reach you. It is one of my greatest pleasures to write.

I took a walk this morning in the public garden [the Alameda] in this city, and how much I wish you had been with me. It is a most lovely spot, more beautiful than any public square I have ever seen in the United States. There are six or eight fine, large fountains, and scores of rose bushes and flowers and shade trees of all kinds. The air is filled with fragrance. The better classes are very fond of flowers, and all must have fountains. Every public square has its fountain and every house which has any pretentions at all has a fountain.

The climate would suit you and me perfectly, for you know I like the northern latitude and you prefer the extreme south. Well, here are two most grand and sublime mountains looking, apparently, down directly upon this city. One of them is Mount Popocatepetl, and the other's name I do not know [Iztaccihuatl], but both are covered with perpetual snow. The former is the [fifth-] highest mountain in North America, and while all the tropical fruits are produced here, the air that comes from the mountains is cool and refreshing.

It would take me a day to show you all the curiosities in this house we now occupy. It is owned by an old man who is very wealthy. He fled into the country when he heard the [American] army was approaching, leaving a steward to take charge of the house. There are hundreds of beautiful flowers in the court, orange trees filled with fruit. The house has its walls covered with paintings; some of them are beautiful, and I have sat many an hour looking at them.

I went a day or two ago with General Worth and some fifty other officers to call on the bishop of the city. He was a very dignified old man with a large ring on his finger and an enormous gold cross around his neck. He showed us through the palace and treated us very politely. Every room through which we passed had many paintings — the walls were literally covered with them — and some of the pieces were of the old Spanish and Italian masters.[1]

But the cathedral is the curiosity in the city.[2] I cannot describe it, but it really surpasses all that I have imagined of St. Peter's at Rome. When I get back, I will give you an account of it. I wish you could hear the enormous organ; it sends forth such thundering peals. But I must tell you of the card I saw posted along the streets. Of course it is in Spanish, but the content of it is as follows: it calls upon the Mexican people to fast, "For neither the wisdom of their rulers nor the valor of their generals has been able to stop the onward progress of the Northern Barbarians." The people are very superstitious, and the priests exercise the most unlimited control over them and make them do as they please.

We hear that Santa Anna has been taken prisoner by another Mexican general whose name I do not recall; but this is certain, there is to be little or no more fighting. Probably at the city of Mexico there will be a few shots fired, but we can take it easy enough. General Scott, we learn, is near, and the whole army will leave soon. When we get to Mexico City, we are at the end of our route, and then if the "powers that be" (if there be any, for they are fighting among themselves there now), do not see fit to treat [for peace], we must wait for our government to decide what is to be done.

I have not had a line from you since we parted and this is my

Panorama of Puebla (Anderson, *An Artillery Officer in the Mexican War,* facing p. 170)

eighth letter. How do you get on with your guitar? Do you play much? Goodbye my dear Kate. May God bless you.

Your affectionate husband.

JOURNAL, May 28, 1847. Puebla.

General Scott arrived today with Colonel Harney's dragoons.[3]

JOURNAL, May 29, 1847. Puebla.

General Twiggs with his division came in today. Paymasters also came, and what was more important and wished for, a large mail from the United States. From this city we have the most grand view of the mountains Popocatepetl and Iztaccihuatl, the former 17,716 [17,887] and the latter 15,700 [17,343] feet above the level of the sea. Both are covered with perpetual snow.

JOURNAL, May 30, 1847. Puebla.

Mr. McCarty, the brigade chaplain, preached today at the 8th Infantry quarters; [his] text, "I would not live always." It was a great pleasure to hear our own beautiful service once more. And yet it was melancholy to me, for it reminded me of the many happy, happy times that I had gone with my dear wife during the past year and taken a part in our own little church at Fort Gibson, and the last time I had the privilege was the Sunday we were together in New Orleans. We went to hear Dr. Hawks and we had the blessed privilege of together kneeling and partaking of the last sacrament instituted by our Savior.[4] The text of Dr. McCarty was very appropriate, for not a day passes but from three to six poor soldiers are carried to their long home and called to from this strange land, far from friends. How many have died since the commencement of this war! And strange as it may seem, officers and soldiers see their companions fall around them daily, apparently without any reflection that their turn may come next. Oh God, prepare me for this event, and may I so live that I may cheerfully obey thy summons when Thou shall see fit to call me!

LETTER, June 1, 1847. Puebla.

My Dearest Kate:

Only think what anniversary this is! It is just a year ago today that we met for the first time, and how many changes have transpired! On the 17th of July we were engaged and the 20th of October we were married. We measure time by events, not by days, months, or years. It seems but yesterday that Flint and myself went down to the boat to welcome you to Fort Gibson.[5] I recall distinctly the events of the day and how I was impressed with you. But it seems to me now that we must always have been together, and yet a year ago today I did not know there was such a little being in existence as Kate Mix! I hardly know myself now. I used to be so fond of seeing everything new; I was ever for detached service of every kind, but now give me my quiet little home that we used to enjoy, and all the glory, honor, scars, and vanities in general I am willing to dispense with.

This morning I took another walk in the Alameda, the beautiful public garden of this city. The band was playing "Home Sweet Home," and I never heard the air when it seemed to fall as it did on my heart.

I must describe the Mexican women for you, how they dress. You rarely see the better classes in the streets, excepting when they go to mass, or on Sunday evening when they ride in the public gardens. Some of the ladies dress with considerable taste, but they never wear bonnets. The only covering for their head is a rebozo or a mantilla. The Mexican women are very graceful, more so than ours; but as for being handsome, or even pretty, it is all a mistake. Nine-tenths of the people resemble the Cherokee Indians as much as possible.

The lower classes, which embrace at least nineteen-twentieths of the whole population, are poor, miserable beings who are as ignorant and superstitious as it is possible to be. The women go barefooted and bareheaded and wear a shawl over their shoulders. They are always smiling and good-natured, working hard, while their husbands are idling their time and spending the few reales which they earn.[6] The majority of the Mexicans seem rather to vegetate than otherwise. The rascally priests live well enough, for they have "the fat of the land" and dress in broadcloth, but you might dress them in rags and it would be easy enough to recognize them by their fat, well-fed bodies. They are a grand set of rogues.

I am so glad you insisted on my bringing a mattress and pillow along with me into the field. I am the envy of many of the officers who had no prudent wife to advise them. And the Spanish grammar you got for me, I am so glad to have it.

You used to beg me not to bring my best horse with me for fear he would break my neck, but he is worth a thousand dollars to me and I would not take anything for him. You know how very fleet he is, and sometimes I have to ride tolerably fast in carrying orders from the head of our brigade to the rear, and, this is quite a distance, sometimes probably two miles. "Rock" is such a noble animal. He is my pride and the envy of a great many cavaliers. My other horse, the sorrel, is not worth much. He was a good horse and a fine traveler, but after taking a great deal of trouble to get him into Mexico, and after I got him as far as Jalapa, he was taken with stiffness in his joints, and I think I shall be obliged to get rid of him.

You wonder how I am getting along without Joseph. Well, rather poorly, for servants are not to be had at any price, and I am sorry I did not take a good black boy with me from New Orleans. I have Burroughs now waiting on me, but he is a soldier, and I do not like to ask him to do many things which I require.

I am afraid to trust the mails here for they are very uncertain with the murderous guerrillas which infest the road all the way from this city to Veracruz. I am awaiting an opportunity to send you some money.

I wish I could present you with some of the beautiful flowers and the fruits you are fond of, particularly oranges and bananas. They are the finest I have ever seen, and the soldiers, particularly the Volunteers, seem to use no discretion, and many are sick. It is a sad sight to see three or four funerals passing by every day, and yet [the men in] the command soon forget it. A great many have been sick from the bad water on the road from Veracruz. I accustomed myself on the march to drink as little as possible.

I hear that the express leaves in the morning and I wish to send this in before it goes. Remember me kindly to all at home. God bless you.

Your ever affectionate husband.

JOURNAL, June 3, 1847. Puebla.

I witnessed today a bullfight, the great amusement of the Spaniards. It took place in a large arena which was built for the purpose. The center is circular, with a diameter of perhaps forty-five or fifty yards. This was enclosed by a wall some six feet in height, over which the men engaged in the exhibition jumped when too closely pressed by the enraged bull. From the wall, six or eight tiers of seats arose one above the others. Around on the outside of this is a circular building of three stories, built of wood. Each story is open towards the arena and is divided into boxes, each box capable of accommodating six or eight individuals. The whole building would conveniently contain, I should judge, at least 5,000 persons.

The Mexicans who were to engage in the scene were dressed in bright, gay dresses, covered with gold and silver laces, very much like the actors of an American circus. The bull was let into the enclosure. There were two persons on horseback [*picadors*]; each had a lance in his hand. There were also five or six on foot; each footman carried in one hand a large piece of dark colored cloth [a cape], which he carried in front of his person, and as the animal would rush at this, he would step [to] one side and thus avoid the danger. As the bull came into the enclosure, a person on one side stuck a large ornament of paper armed with pointed steel into his neck; this made him somewhat furious. Then each one rushed up, shaking their cloths in his face. The animal, being in an enclosure, surrounded by thousands of persons shouting or clapping their hands, and a band playing all

A Sunday bullfight (Albert S. Evans, *Our Sister Republic: A Gala Trip through Tropical Mexico* [Hartford, Conn., 1870], p. 145)

the time, felt somewhat frightened, and then with [the] bright cloths thrust into his face, made him furious. Occasionally, one of the party [a *banderillero*] would thrust into him some sharp piece of metal, on the end of which were attached firecrackers. Their exploding would frighten and make him still more furious. Pretty soon one of the horsemen would thrust his spear into him, and the more the poor animal was tortured, the more the spectators seemed to enjoy it. The bull was finally dispatched by one of the most skillful of the performers [the *torero*], who, with one thrust of his sword, stabbed him to the heart. Mules were driven in and the dead body dragged out.

In a few minutes another bull was driven in, and the same performance went through with. I witnessed three and was quite satisfied with bullfights. It is certainly the most cruel amusement that I ever witnessed. Not only the poor animals are thus cruelly butchered, but

23

the persons are in danger of not only being gored and perhaps having their limbs broken, but are in actual danger of their lives. I saw one poor fellow who was unhorsed by the bull, which rushed upon him as he came into the enclosure, and he was carried out by his companions, either dead or nearly so. Still, the spectators shouted and seemed to enjoy it very much. In fact, the scene was more or less exciting, according as the performers were in more or less danger.

LETTER, June 5, 1847. Puebla.

Dear Katie:

At last I have heard from you. On the arrival of the mail this morning I received three letters, Nos. 1, 2, and 3. You cannot imagine my delight, and I shall have to read them over and over for we are so far from the [Gulf] Coast now that the possibility of getting and sending letters is somewhat uncertain. But I shall write regularly as before, even if you do not get all my letters.

I think the war cannot last much longer. [Rumors say that] Santa Anna has abdicated and General Bravo and some others have resigned.[7] So there will be no more fighting; that is, we all think so. There are no fortifications on the road or in Mexico City, so we can march there if we please tomorrow; but we are comfortably fixed here and the climate is perfectly delightful.

I am regaining my rosy cheeks and have gained some five or six pounds. I was talking with some priests a few days ago, and they asked me how old I was. I told them, but they would not believe me. They said I was only twenty. And you say my daguerreotype looks cross. Well, these daguerreotypes do not flatter; it must be my natural look. But I have in my pocket one [of you] so smiling and cheerful that I look at it many times and would not part with it for anything. There is a man in Mexico City who takes pictures, and if I get there, I will call on him.

I must not forget to tell you that I have attended a bullfight a day or two ago. One sight is sufficient, and yet there were young ladies, mothers and daughters to see this cruel sport. They had four bulls brought into the arena, one after the other. Each was killed after being cruelly tortured for a long time by lances, spears, and firecrackers which were attached to them by pointed pieces of steel. I will give you an account of it when I get home. It was really curious to one

24

unaccustomed to such sights. But how any person can enjoy anything of this kind is more than I can see.

My duties now are very pleasant and I have more leisure. We have a chaplain to our brigade. Last Sunday, however, was the first time he has been able to preach. It was a great joy to hear our service here in this distant country. His text was, "I would not live always," which is so appropriate here as many of the command are dying, that is among the soldiers. Not a day passes but I see from one to four or even five funerals pass by my quarters, and a military funeral never loses its solemnity; daily some poor fellow goes to his long home.

I received a few lines from your brother William. He was at Brazos Island. I shall write him soon.[8]

I must tell you that I traded off the sorrel horse, for he was of no use to me. I gave $10.00 to boot and got a good horse, for a Mexican horse.

Please send me some newspapers; and the *Christian Witness,* I would very much like to have.

I shall be heartily glad when the war is over and we can sit down to our own fireside and obtain the only perfect happiness which is to be had in this world. For certainly if it is to be obtained here, it is by our own hearth. I am forming many projects for the future. Goodbye.

Ever your affectionate husband.

JOURNAL, June 6, 1847. Puebla.

Dr. McCarty preached twice today. In the morning, at the 8th Infantry quarters, text: 95th Psalm, 6th verse: "Oh come, let us worship and bow down; let us kneel before the Lord our maker." In the afternoon, service was held at General Scott's quarters, text: I Corinthians, 13th chapter, 10, 11, 12 verses. There were quite a number of officers attended, and I was glad to see that many of them went through all the forms and apparently were interested in the service. How beautiful it is, and peculiarly so in this strange land. Today when we came to the "Gloria in excelsis," Major [John L.] Gardner, 4th Artillery, commenced chanting it in a clear, deep and rich voice. Several other officers immediately joined in, and I never felt more devotional and more grateful to my Kind Heavenly Father than I did at that moment. Here we were far, far away from our native land, surrounded by these idolatrous Mexicans, who look upon every one of us as a heretic; here in this foreign land was heard our church service. Next Sunday our chaplain intends to administer the sacrament of the Lord's supper. Oh how fortunate I am! What cause I have for the deepest gratitude to God, for his daily blessing which he is bestowing upon me!

The following are the distances from Veracruz to the City of Mexico. From Veracruz to:

Santa Fé	3 leagues
Puente Nacional	8 leagues
Plan del Río	6 leagues
Jalapa	8 leagues
Las Vigas	7 leagues
Perote	4 leagues
Tepeyahualco	7 leagues
Ojo de Agua	6 leagues
Napoluca	2 leagues
Amozoc	8 leagues
Puebla	3 leagues
San Martín	8 leagues
Río Frío	8 leagues
[Buena Vista]	5 leagues
Mexico [City]	10 leagues

Total 93 leagues [1 league equaled 2.6 miles]

LETTER, June 6, 1847. Puebla.

My Dear Wife:

I sent you a letter only yesterday, but it is Sunday evening and I have been sitting more than an hour by myself, thinking of those who are far away. I have been twice today to church and what a treat it was! Mr. McCarty gave out some hymns and we sang "Old Hundredth" [Praise God, from whom all blessings flow] and "Hebron" [Eternal Son, eternal love]. This is a blessing which I did not expect in this country. Our brigade is the only one with General Scott that has a chaplain. We had service this afternoon at General Scott's quarters, and he was present and went through the service.

Here, Sunday is the day of all the seven for amusements. Everybody goes to mass on Sunday in the morning. To be sure, there are at least one hundred churches open daily in this city, and in each one of them mass is said from one to four times.[9] Yet on Sunday even those persons who cannot or do not attend on weekdays go, and in the afternoon and evening the streets are crowded by persons going to places of amusements. The theaters are open and the bullfight is better attended than any other day. Another place of amusement in this city is the Tivoli Garden where all meet to dance.

On the 3rd of this month there was a grand celebration here. It was called Corpus Christi Day.[10] Instead, however, of bearing the host through the streets as usual, it was dispensed with, as the priests were afraid that many of our troops would not kneel as they passed in the streets, but the processions were formed in the churches. Many of our officers attended. Some took wax candles in their hands and followed on in the train, but I could not do this. I believe the more I see of the Romish religion in this country, the more I am convinced that it is real idolatry. The great mass of the people, which comprises nineteen-twentieths of the whole, are kept in a state of perfect ignorance. The whole church service is performed in Latin; of course they understand nothing of it. They go to mass once, twice, or three times a week, repeat a Latin prayer which has been taught them, cross themselves, beat their breasts, kiss the floor, and all their sins are forgiven, and the individual is ready to commit any new crime that may offer itself. To show you what a dread the people have for anything heretical and how superstitious they are: if a Mexican buys an American horse, or becomes possessed of one, he pays the priest a round sum to baptize [bless] it.

LETTER, June 7, 1847. Puebla.

My Dearest Kate:

The mail is in and I have received [your] two letters, Numbers 4 and 5, one from New Orleans and the last on the boat going to Alton. I also had a letter from my father, one from brother Albert, one from each of my sisters Frances and Jeanette, one from Colonel Loomis, one from Captain Ogden, and one from your brother Alfred.[11] So many letters at once is almost overwhelming; at least Colonel Clarke thought so, for it happened the mail came just as Colonel Clarke was getting his brigade ready for a grand parade, review, and inspection, which takes place tomorrow under General Worth. Of course, he had a hundred orders to give me, and he would be telling me where this regiment was to go, etc., and I was trying to read a line or two of your letters. But at last I mounted my horse to go to the different regiments of our brigade. I started at full gallop and did not stop until I got out of town. Then I could enjoy my letters uninterruptedly.

Letter, June 8, 1847. Puebla.

Well, we had our grand review, parade, and inspection today. There is no parade ground in the city large enough for more than one regiment, so we went out about a mile, and there we found a place where all of General Scott's army could drill. We had there together six regiments, and there was plenty of room. Colonel Hitchcock is inspecting general, and he inspected the troops.[12] General Worth took the review. He is a splendid officer in every respect, but with all his experience he does not understand marching an army. But I will not enter into the merits of the case.

Where is your little brother Gussey [Gustave L. Mix] this summer? Poor fellow, did he not have a hard time of it at Fort Gibson? He used to annoy me exceedingly a year ago. You recollect, don't you? All of Colonel Loomis' family kept an eye on me as if they suspected I was going to steal something [you]. They weren't in the wrong either. But I will never do so again.

General Scott says that we may rest assured of our going out of Mexico in October next, and you know, should the war close, it would be important to leave before then on account of the *vómito* [yellow fever], which prevails as late as that month at Veracruz.

I wish you would send me something to read, I am so fond of reading. Send anything that you can; cut out pieces from the papers and put them in an envelope. I have got all the letters so far. I am very thankful for that.

Letter, June 10, 1847. Puebla.

I began this letter some days ago, but as there is no mail leaving I will continue to write you.

We have been out all the afternoon, from 3 until 7, drilling. We are making considerable of a stay here. General Worth is improving the time in getting his division in first-rate order.

I miss my flute very much, but I had no room to bring it. I left it with my trunk and nearly everything else at Veracruz, but I have written to the quartermaster to send my trunk by the first train that comes up. You cannot hear from me in the future, I fear, as often as formerly, for we are far in the interior and there is no telling when an opportunity will offer to send letters. There was an interval of twenty days between the last two mails, and it is very uncertain when we shall get another. But continue to write.

LETTER, June 11, 1847. Puebla.

I saw a man this morning who left Mexico City day before yesterday. He says there are about 16,000 men [Mexican soldiers] there. Santa Anna has got Generals Arista, Ampudia, and Almonte under arrest.[13] General [Nicolás] Bravo is in command of a height [El Peñón] some four leagues this side of the city, which he is fortifying. Santa Anna has 5,000 men from the south, called "Pintos" [contemptible ones], or some such name. They are armed with an instrument used in tilling the soil and now converted into a bludgeon. They are considered very dangerous by the Mexicans. A round of grape [cluster of iron balls fired by a cannon] would soon send these Pintos home again.

The Mexicans have got a report out among them that we are at war with England and will soon withdraw from Mexico. Their leaders circulate the most outrageous lies among the people. For several days before we came here and before the main army had arrived, it was reported and believed that General Scott had died at Perote or Jalapa.

JOURNAL, June 12, 1847. Puebla.

General Worth reviewed and drilled his division today. Our brigade has been preparing for it for several days past, and the sight today was indeed magnificent. The troops formed in line extended more than half a mile in length, and in passing in review we marched at least three miles. There were the 4th, 5th, 6th, & 8th Regiments of Infantry, Colonel Smith's light battalion, the 2nd & 3rd Regiment of Artillery, and several companies of light artillery on the field. The day has been somewhat warm; we went out soon after 7 o'clock and it was 2 before we got home.[14]

LETTER, June 12, 1847. Puebla.

Well, this week has closed. I am very tired. We have been drilling, having reviews and inspections all the week. Today we were reviewed by General Worth, and it was a most splendid sight. We had seven regiments on the ground, besides our artillery. Our line was upwards of half a mile when formed, and when passing in review, we marched at least three miles. I never beheld a more magnificent sight.

JOURNAL, June 13, 1847. Puebla.

Today again have I been permitted to go to the house of God, and there with others who profess to love Him, offer up our prayers and praises. After morning service, we had a sacrament of the Lord's supper administered. It was very solemn; I knelt. The last time I was permitted this privilege with my dearest little wife; today I was alone, and when we shall be permitted to kneel again, as we were accustomed to do side by side, my Heavenly Father alone knows. It was very gratifying to see so many officers from different corps and regiments kneeling together and confessing their love to their Creator. Oh may my kind Parent, who has ever blessed me thus far, extend his protecting hand over His precious gift to His unworthy servant. Thou hast given me, oh God, my dearest companion, my own dear wife. She is Thy gift, and I thank Thee for her. She has taught me, by her gentleness, her amiability and purity of character, to be a better man myself, to be more generous, more pure, and less selfish. And Heavenly Father, watch over her, I pray Thee, and in Thine own due time restore her to her devoted husband. Oh God, may we ever be to each other as we are now, may our love increase in purity and holiness as long as [we] are blessed in each other's society. And may we both so live, that when we are called to leave this world, we shall go together to praise Thee in Heaven. I ask this in my Redeemer's name! Amen.

LETTER, June 15, 1847. Puebla.

I do not know when I can send this letter off. No train is going out of the country for a long time. There is a rumor that there is a large Mexican force in our rear, and we have no troops to send as escort which could resist an attack of from six to eight thousand of the enemy.

I will not write more in this letter. God grant we may soon meet. Goodbye.

Your ever affectionate husband.

LETTER, June 17, 1847. Puebla.

Dear Katie:

It is only a few days since I wrote you and I have nothing new to communicate, but I have been thinking that this is your birthday, and so I am sending a few lines. How much I wish I was with you! It requires all my faculties of cheerfulness to get along without murmuring. But "Hope on; hope ever," that is our motto.

There is a great deal of wickedness in this world, and particularly when so large a body is collected together as there is in our army, and especially so during the war. I cannot describe the amount of wickedness in the way of profanity, sabbath-breaking, intemperance, and gambling which is daily practiced with the army and the army followers. Temptation in every form is being presented to the army. There is a circus, a theater, and a set of gamblers which follow in our train, and naturally these dens are all open and hundreds frequent them, Sunday being no exception. In fact, this day of the Sabbath is selected to offer the greatest attraction, and there is a bullfight every Sunday.

I am pretty busy. I do not know when we shall go on, but probably in the course of a week or ten days. You must not look for letters often, for all communications will soon be closed and probably not more than once a month will opportunities offer for sending letters. This goes by a Mexican, who leaves in the morning for Veracruz, but there are so many robberies on the road that even Mexicans are robbed and murdered.

I am still enjoying perfect health and think I shall escape all sickness. We are looking for Captain Lovell in about four or five days. I shall be glad to see him for he saw you just before he left.[15]

I do not know what I shall do about sending you money. I would, if I dared, send you a check in this letter. The last Mexican papers have letters in them which were captured by the enemy. One is from Colonel Childs's wife to him.[16] Only think of them getting our letters from our wives and friends in the United States, and not only depriving us of them, but publishing them in their papers!

Goodbye my dear wife.

Ever your truly affectionate husband.

Journal, June 24, 1847. Puebla.

Today is Saint John's [St. John the Baptist's] day and is celebrated by the Romanists [Roman Catholics]. It is considered also, I believe, a holy day. In the morning all the churches in the city were open, and everybody attended. I went into some three or four. The cathedral first attracted me; here I was sure of hearing some good music. I remained there about two hours, the organ playing most of the time. There were also several instruments accompanying it. I could distinguish violins, a trombone, French horn, flutes, etc. The music resembled an opera as much as anything else. I remained and saw the "elevation of the host."

The day was ushered in by the firing off of rockets, which commenced as early as three o'clock in the morning, and at daybreak the bells began to ring. In the afternoon the ladies were out in their coaches in the Alameda, and most of the young men were prancing about on their horses. Those who had neither coach nor horse put on their best clothes and smiling faces, and joined the crowd, for happy they were determined to be.

It is now the rainy season, and rarely a day passes without a shower in the afternoon, and some days the sky is cloudy and rain falls with intermissions during the twenty-four hours. But generally, the nights are clear and cold. The mornings are bright and beautiful. Towards eleven or twelve o'clock, the sun grows pretty warm, and at three the clouds begin to rise, and by four or five the rain falls, and at seven or eight the heavens are clear again. This is the case four days out of five.

Journal, June 28, 1847. Puebla.

I witnessed today the funeral of a little girl about eight years of age. I saw the procession coming down the street as I was standing on the balcony in the second story of my quarters. The procession was led by some ten or twelve boys who carried long, lighted wax candles;

then came some dozen or ten persons, chiefly females and children who were probably friends of the family; then came a priest in full robes; after him was the coffin, but the top was off, and the little girl was lying, as it were, in a bed of flowers. The coffin was invisible from the number of flowers; it was covered as well on the outside as in. The little girl was dressed in her gayest clothes, her hands were crossed on her bosom, and her fair face wore a sweet smile. I could hardly believe the child was dead.

The coffin was borne by four little boys about her own age. After the corpse, came the child's mother and two or three children who, from their grief, appeared to be her brother and sisters. The procession was brought up by some twenty persons who seemed to have joined in the street. But one thing I noticed, almost all present had a handful of flowers and were smiling as though they were going on some pleasure excursion. After reaching the church, under the floor of which a grave had been prepared, the procession formed around the coffin, which had been placed beside the grave, and the funeral service was read. And the little girl was shut up in her narrow house, and a few minutes more and all had gone. I lingered a little while, yielding to the sad reflections which such an occasion called forth.

I have every day remarked the great fondness of the Mexicans for flowers. You can scarcely find a house without some few, and many, even of the poorer classes, have a great variety. Most of the houses have balconies or projections from the windows in which they usually keep their flower pots and vases, and as the temperature in this latitude is equable, they require little care besides watering in the dry season.

The Mexicans are also passionately fond of birds, not only singing birds, but a variety of others. Mocking and canary birds are very common; the former can be bought when young for a mere trifle, sometimes as low as 12½ cents [one *real*]. And I have seen old songsters, which would have sold for ten and twenty dollars in the United States, here offered for one or two dollars. The Mexicans seem to value them as pets. I have gone into a house of the low order of people and counted as many as ten cages, each with one and some with two birds, and perhaps some half a dozen others were perched in different parts of the room. I have also frequently noticed cats, which seemed to be on familiar terms with them, but never offered them any violence.

One other passion the Mexicans have and gratify is that for paintings and pictures. I will venture to say there is not a house or a room occupied by Mexicans in the city of Puebla which has not from one to twenty paintings and engravings. Of course many and the greater portion of them are daubs, yet there are many fine oil paintings, and all, without any exception, are on religious subjects. Most of them are heads or half lengths, and are either our Saviour or more probably the Virgin and Child.

LETTER, June 28, 1847. Puebla.

My Dear Wife:

I am so impatient to hear of your arrival at Alton and that you are safe and happy with [your] sister Sophie. I wish there was something known when we could expect to leave this country, but as yet everything is obscure. The Mexicans have no inclination to treat [for peace], and even after we are in possession of the City of Mexico I do not see that the war is any nearer to a close. I have been anxiously awaiting an opportunity to safely send you some money, but none presents itself.

In a few days we look for a train and mail, and I am so anxious to hear from you. I understand the train brings mail from New Orleans as late as the 1st of June. I wonder if you get all my letters. I write often enough.

I wish you would try to send me some papers. I have little or nothing to read. I found some of [Sir Walter] Scott's novels here some few days since, and I have read *The Bride of Lammermoor, Ivanhoe,* and *Kenilworth.* My library consists of *Army Regulations,* [Winfield] Scott's [Infantry] *Tactics,* my *Bible, Book of Prayer,* and *Spanish Dictionary.* I wrote you that I had left my trunk at Veracruz and hope to get it in the course of a month, if the enemy does not catch it.

We have been here six weeks [awaiting reinforcements and trying to negotiate a peace], and still General Scott has not decided when he will go on. We have maps of our route and know the topography of the country between this city and Mexico City. Our troops are in splendid order. If we have any more fighting we shall have a larger force than ever. We have just heard that General Pillow has landed at Veracruz and sent on an express to General Cadwalader, who is still in Perote, to remain there until he comes up.[17] So we cannot leave here for still a longer time. We shall have more troops, as many as General Scott wishes.

I am still doing duty of assistant adjutant general to the 2nd brigade of General Worth's division; also I do my duty as adjutant to my colonel. When the generals in the rear come up, it is possible that Colonel Clarke will be relieved of command of the brigade and take immediate command of his regiment. In that case, I shall also be relieved of the duties I now perform, but I shall not care, for it does not give me any extra pay although it doubles my duties. The only advantages I have would be in case of a battle I should have greater advantages to distinguish myself.

I must say goodbye now, somewhat reluctantly, but I will write soon again, and I hope before long to get letters from you. Remember me kindly to all the family. Goodbye. God bless you.

Your ever affectionate husband.

JOURNAL, July 4, 1847. Puebla.

Today, being the anniversary of our national Independence, has been kept in a variety of ways, but as a general thing the soldiers have been very orderly. Not much drinking. The theater and circus have been open, and this evening there is to be a grand ball, to be attended, so the cards say, by a number of the Mexican ladies.

But to those who prefer to keep the day [Sunday] holy, as it should be kept, the opportunity was offered. We had divine service twice, and in the morning the holy sacrament of the Lord's Supper was administered. There were sixteen officers who partook, a very small proportion of the great number in the city. Among them were Major Waite; Dr. Tripler; Captain Taylor, 1st Artillery; Captains Smith, Penrose, and Davidson, 2nd Infantry; Captain Hanson, 7th Infantry; Lieutenants Lindsay, Stone, Nichols, Anderson, Martin; and Captain Roberts, Rifles. It is a great blessing to be permitted, so far away from home and in an enemy's country, to be permitted to join, and probably at the same hour, with hundreds and thousands in this divine institution.[18]

I could not but think today that, perhaps at the same time with myself, my own dearest wife was similarly engaged, and I know that, whilst I was offering up my prayers for her that God would smile upon her and grant her His choice blessings, she was praying for her absent husband, little thinking that he was so blessed. Oh God! May I realize the importance of leading a new life, and may I strive to be more true and Christian-like, in my thoughts, words, and actions. May I constantly bear in mind that I profess to be a Christian, and may my daily intercourse with my associates promote this cause rather than cast a slur on it. May I, by my kindness and courtesy to all, recommend the religion which I profess to love.

JOURNAL, July 17, 1847. Puebla.

This is the anniversary of the engagement of myself and my little wife. One year ago today we exchanged our vows, and I can say with sincerity that during this year which has just closed, I have hardly experienced an unhappy moment. After our engagement, we passed nearly nine months together, six of them as husband and wife. What happiness there exists in this endearing relation. None but those who have enjoyed its blessings can appreciate it. I was happy when I had my beloved Kate with me, and even in separation I enjoy a satisfaction that I never felt before, for Hope, blessed Hope, is constantly whispering of joys yet to come. I know there is one being and she the one whom I selected of all others as being best calculated in disposition to make me happy. She, I know, is devoted to me, and daily, yes hourly, offers up her prayers at the throne of grace for my welfare. I cannot but love her tenderly, devotedly, for she has been given to me by my kind Heavenly Father, and I trust I shall love and cherish her with all the devotion of which she is so justly deserving. And I sincerely pray that the same kind Parent, who entrusted this precious gift in my charge, will in His own due time restore her to my heart.

I went today, in company with some one or two hundred other officers, and visited the celebrated pyramid of Cholula. We had an escort of the 4th Regiment of Artillery and a squadron of dragoons. The town of Cholula lies a little south of west from Puebla and is about three leagues [7.8 miles] distant. The ancient city is in ruins. It was at one time very extensive; the population now is about six or eight thousand. A great portion of the ground upon which formerly stood squares inhabited by thousands of people are now fields of corn. The pyramid seems to stand in the center of what was the city. It is artificial, made of earth and unburned brick. It very irregular in con-

Cholula and the Ancient Pyramid (Albert S. Evans, *Our Sister Republic: A Gala Trip through Tropical Mexico* [Hartford, Conn., 1870], p. 428)

tour and is covered on its sides by shrubs and trees; a winding pathway leads to its summit, which is level, with an area of perhaps fifty by eighty yards. Here stands an ancient church, built by the Spaniards in 1666, so says the date on the walls. This chapel is still used and is in a good state of preservation.[19]

The view from the tower is very extensive and picturesque. You have before you, extending for miles, a plain under high cultivation, and it is remarkably fertile and rich. No less than twenty or thirty haciendas are in sight, and some of them are extensive enough to be regarded as small towns or villages. Many of the officers bought little articles of Mexican manufacture, from a family which lives in a room adjoining the church, to take home as curiosities. But I gathered a handful of flowers and got an old book in Spanish, which has been used in the church; it is a manual of devotion. We rode through the town, which lies at the base of the pyramid, but there was little of interest there. We had a delightful day and returned to Puebla by one o'clock P.M.

I have been spending the evening with some other officers at the home of a Mexican officer who treated us very agreeably. There were several ladies present who sang and played upon the harp and guitar for us and danced the polka and a variety of other dances for us. We had the 6th Infantry band in the street in front of the house, which added to our enjoyment. We returned home about ten o'clock and were much gratified with our evening's entertainment. But when and with whom shall I pass the next anniversary of my engagement? With my darling wife I hope and pray, and in our own quiet home.

JOURNAL, July 22, 1847. Puebla.

I attended the Spanish [language] theater this evening. The performance was very good as far as I could judge, for I could understand but little of the language. There was a very amusing Spanish song called "La Morena" [The Brunette], and the evening closed with the comedy of "The Mysteries of a Minor." The actors knew their parts very well, and to those who could follow the plot, it must have been quite amusing. The orchestra was excellent, and the music alone was sufficient to pay one for going.

JOURNAL, August 1, 1847. Puebla.

I have been to church all day and this morning was permitted to partake of the holy communion. It was a very solemn ceremony. I could not but think that at the same time that I was kneeling at the sacred table, those whom I love, far, far away in the United States were doing likewise; that whilst I was not only praying for myself, but for the blessing of God upon my dearest wife, she was perhaps praying at the same holy place for her absent husband. I feel nearer to her upon occasions of this kind than at any other. When I am alone, particularly, and am offering up my prayers in her behalf, I rise from my knees full of happiness, confident that she is well and happy, and that the good Angels of Heaven are watching over her, and that in God's own due time we shall again be permitted to meet.

It rained again this afternoon, quite hard in fact; the interval from rain which we have enjoyed for the past two weeks has ceased and we now have a shower, and a heavy one too, daily. These rains are to continue, I understand, for some six or seven weeks, and then the rainy season closes.

One regiment (the 8th) of our brigade left this morning on a foraging expedition — to be gone some five or six days. One brigade of Gen.

Twiggs's division has also gone out on detached service to meet General Pierce and come up with him.[20]

LETTER, August 1, 1847. Puebla.

My Dearest Wife:

You see we are still in this city, although when I last wrote you it was believed we should be in the neighborhood of Mexico City before this time. However, it is all for the best, and in a few days I hope to hear from you, for General Pierce, we learn, is at Perote and ought to be here in about five days. How anxiously I am looking for him for I have only received your seven letters, [the last] written the week after you arrived at Alton, and you have now been there two months and a half.

We are still in doubts about going on [to Mexico City]. Rumors are various but there is a general opinion that we shall go next week. We shall move then, or we shall not do so for six or eight weeks. When General Pierce arrives, General Scott will either start immediately or dispatch a train back to Veracruz for our ammunition for the siege train, which is rather short. We have but 250 shells; we ought to have at least 1,000, but the bayonet is the effective weapon, General Scott says.

LETTER, August 3, 1847. Puebla.

I was agreeably surprised last night by the arrival of the mail which came in advance of the troops under escort of Mexican Rascals.[21] General Scott has in employ these men; having them well paid they are true to us. I received no less than six letters, from Number 7 up to 13. So you see, none of your letters have been lost; they are all in my hands. You must not worry about me. I am not sleeping on the cold, bare ground; I have a first-rate camp bed which, with my mattress and bedding, makes me very comfortable.

I hope to be able to get a furlough, should the war close. I have had it promised me by Colonel Clarke. My appointment as acting assistant adjutant general is not permanent, and as soon as there is peace, we shall be assigned to stations in different parts of our country. I shall go with the 6th Regiment. What is very probable is we shall be stationed in very desirable posts. The 6th has been so long in the Indian country it deserves a better set of posts.

I presume a good many of my letters have fallen into the hands of the Mexicans, but it cannot be helped. I received some papers from you last night, also a recipe for the foundered horse, but it came too late. "Rock" is a splendid animal and has settled down, as I ride him so much, but still he has lost none of his fleetness, and should I have occasion, I could trust him against any horse in this country. I would not part with him for anything.

I believe Major Woods is with the troops which are expected in a few days. I shall be glad to see him for he has seen you, and besides he is an old friend of mine.[22]

You seem to express considerable anxiety lest I should become a Romanist [Roman Catholic]. Have no fears on that subject for I assure you I am less one now than I was before I came to this country. I have seen too much wickedness among those who profess this faith to change my church. We [you and I] are blessed with the same holy religion, and I trust we and our descendants will ever be firm supporters of it.

I have been out riding through the city, getting the news of the day. But there is nothing of a train going to Veracruz yet, and the general opinion is that until Mexico City is taken, none will go. I hope all communication will be kept open and letters come and go with some regularity.

LETTER, August 6, 1847. Puebla.

We are at last packing up, and Monday next, the 9th of the month, we are off for the Halls of the Montezumas. The order for the going-out march is as follows: General Twiggs starts first, to the disappointment of our division; next comes General Pillow, and then General Worth. General Twiggs with his division leaves tomorrow, and there is an interval of one day between each division. There are many opinions as to whether we shall have another fight; some predict that not a shot will be fired. But we are ready for anything, that is, we are in fine fighting order, and General Scott will do the thing up in the most scientific order.

I do not know when this letter will start as no train leaves until we reach Mexico City. Well, I will say goodbye and write again in a few days.

Ever your affectionate husband.

JOURNAL, August 8, 1847. Puebla.

Today has been a very busy day, making arrangements for moving on [toward Mexico City] in the morning. We start at 6 o'clock. Colonel Clarke inspected his entire brigade this morning. I have felt all day the need of quiet, for of all days, Sunday is the one on which we wish to be free from cares, but today has been the most busy of the season. General Twiggs moved on with his division on Saturday, General Quitman started with his today, and tomorrow General Worth leaves this city. We have been here twelve weeks, and it will be three months tomorrow since we left Perote. We left there on Sunday, the 9th of May, and on Monday, the 9th of August, we leave Puebla.

We go looking for a very sure action in the course of a few days. We have been in a doubtful state for some time, whether we should go on or remain here until the rainy season is over. But now it is decided, and we are to go. All are anxious to meet the enemy and march into the capital of the country. If we do fight, many an honest and brave heart that now beats will beat no more. We must expect to go with our lives, as it were, in our hands, ready if called upon to lay them down for our country.

Oh God, I put my trust in Thee. Thou has ever been my support, and the same Providence which has smiled upon me thus far through life will still rule. Whatever may be Thy disposition of this unworthy servant, I say, "Thy will be done." But oh God, bless my dearest, my beloved Kate. I love her, Thou knowest, more than all the world beside. She is Thy dearest, most precious gift to me, and I have fondly hoped to spend many a bright happy year with her. Thou also knowest if I am to realize those hopes. I profess to love Thee, but I am very wicked, unworthy to have a companion so gentle, so pure, and so lovely. But my Father, since Thou hast given her to me, to influence me, to make me more pure and less selfish, to be, as it were, my guardian angel through life, I have, I trust, tried to be worthy of her. Into Thy hands I commit her and willingly and cheerfully, too. As for myself, my kind Parent, prepare me for the worst. If I am to bid farewell to all held dear on earth, may I do so "not like the galley slave who goes scourged to his dungeon, but like one who wraps the drapery of his couch around him and lies down to pleasant dreams."

CHAPTER THREE

Battles for Mexico City

JOURNAL, August 9, 1847. Río Prieto.

Our march has been from Puebla to this place today. We started about 7 o'clock and arrived here about half past one, distance four leagues. It was cool and pleasant until about 12 when the sun became quite warm.

The country over which we have passed is beautiful, highly cultivated with corn, beans, and peppers, and large plantations of the maguey or Agave Americana. We are now much nearer the volcanoes of Puebla [Popocatepetl and Iztaccihuatl] than we have been before; they seem to be within ten miles. The sky has been very clear and Orizaba [the peak] has also been distinctly visible all day.[1] It is now, just at retreat, preparing for a rainy night; but as the dust has been inconvenient all day, we are not sorry to see it, although we have but few tents to protect our men and arms.

JOURNAL, August 10, 1847. San Martín [Texmelucan].

We arrived here at 6 o'clock, having marched 4 leagues. It is quite a village. The country is beautiful, fields of corn extending miles along the road. We had quite a stampede at night. The alarm was given and, although a shower came up just at the time, the troops were under arms some time. But at last no one seemed to know what had caused the disturbance. We managed to find shelter for most of the troops in the houses of the place.

JOURNAL, August 11, 1847. Río Frío.

We marched from San Martín to Río Frío, distance 7 leagues. We had a long and fatiguing march as our brigade was behind the train, and the road being very steep in many places, and the mules poor, we did not get into camp until after dark and after having been in the rain for some two hours. The first brigade had been in camp two hours at least. Río Frío is a small place, not more than a dozen houses. The elevation is so great that we had a frost at night. The water is ice cold and very pure. The troops all slept out for want of shelter, and although we were able to get plenty of wood and water, still the men suffered. I had to get up at two o'clock in the morning to detail a company for picket guard. This kept me up an hour, and having a bad cold, I rose the next morning somewhat indisposed.

JOURNAL, August 12, 1847. Chalco.

We marched today 7½ leagues, passing Llano Grande, Baranca de Quana, Venta de Córdova, the hacienda de Buena Vista (where we found General Quitman with his division), and Ventilla. Here we took the road to the left of the lake [Lake Chalco] and marched nearly south abreast of the lake to this town. Before we got here we had orders from General Scott, who had gone on to Ayotla, to take possession of this place. He had information that it was in possession of some two or three thousand Mexican troops, and we must dislodge them at once. Well, we were expecting a fight, but on getting near the town, we found the enemy had vamoosed this morning. We marched in and found quarters for the division.

We are now on the west of the volcanoes of Puebla, and the view of Popocatepetl is, if anything, even more beautiful and grand than from Puebla. The view as we left Río Frío [for] some four or six miles was very extensive and the most beautiful I ever saw. We had the entire valley of the city of Mexico, extending miles in every direction, dotted here and there with villages and haciendas, and the lakes were visible, reaching even to the city itself, but the city was hidden by hills.[2] The lakes are nothing but stagnant duck ponds, the surface is covered with tall grass reeds and water lilies; yet hundreds of boats are seen, passing in different directions, loaded with fruits, vegetables, etc. The country through which we passed yesterday and [the] day before is very fertile, and under a good government the people ought to be rich, contented and healthy. And [in] a beautiful country this perfect, men now are living, nine-tenths of them, from hand to mouth, dependent upon their masters almost for everything they have.

43

JOURNAL, August 13, 1847. Chalco.

We have remained all day at Chalco. General Scott came over from General Twiggs's camp this morning. General Worth had just started out with his commanders for the purpose of looking about the neighborhood, etc., when he heard of General Scott's arrival. Of course our ride was given up, and we returned to town. General Scott remained about an hour; he said he had not fully decided upon his plan, etc., but would have done so by the 15th. He has had reconnoitering parties out for the past two days. El Peñón is strongly fortified; the engineers report that it can be taken, but with considerable loss of life.[3] Then we gain but little, as the road for miles is on the causeway with water on both sides. General Scott, in speaking of his movements, said he should use the utmost moderation and prudence, sparing his command as much as possible; that if a place could be taken, it should be done with the minimum loss of life, that every man above that who should be lost, he should consider himself responsible for.

General Quitman came up with his division this afternoon and took up quarters in the south part of the town.

JOURNAL, August 14, 1847. Chalco.

We remain still at Chalco. Parties have been out all day in different directions reconnoitering. Colonel Duncan went about two-thirds of the way to Xochimilco and reports an excellent road; [he] saw no Mexicans. A party went out last night [under] Lieutenant Hamilton who went to obtain some information at Miraflores, where there is a foundry. [He] was very severely wounded; he was in advance of the infantry with some forty dragoons. The party was surrounded by guerrillas, and he was lanced in his back whilst in the act of cutting down a Mexican in front of him. He was brought in this morning, and his wound is very dangerous, perhaps mortal.[4]

JOURNAL, August 15, 1847. Chalco.

Sunday morning. We have been here now three days, and probably before another twenty-four hours go by, we shall be on the march, and before another Sunday returns, we shall be in the city of Mexico. And one alone can tell how many of those who are now in the vigor

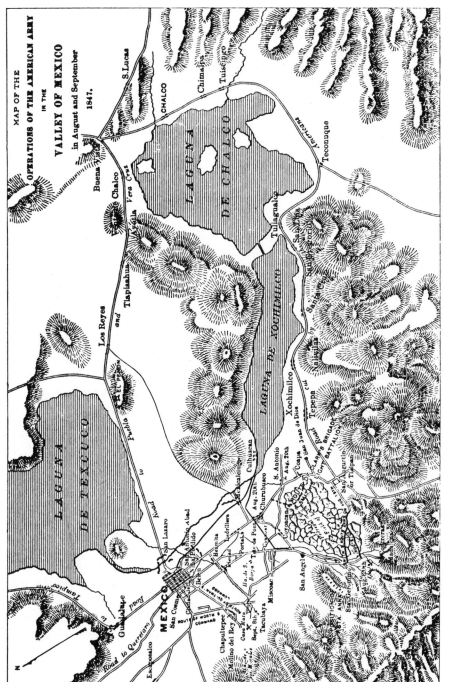

Campaigns in the Valley of Mexico (from Santa Anna, *The Eagle*, p. 175)

45

of life will see its return. This is the day when I think most of those whom I love, and although I cannot tell how my friends are engaged on other days of the week, on this day I know they are employed in religious duties. My dearest wife, I know, will wonder how I am getting along, and whether I am permitted to join in the prayers and praises of the church, but we are not thus permitted today. I hope I shall keep the day as holy as circumstances will permit, and I trust the time will soon return when I can observe this day in the blessed retirement of a quiet home.

LETTER, August 22, 1847. Tacubaya.

My Dearest Wife:

I felt confident when I last wrote you that we would have some fighting before I could write again. I also felt quite confident that I should be protected and brought safely through all danger. I cannot give you the details or even an outline of our camps from Puebla to this place, for it is two weeks since we marched, and every day has been crowded with incidents of more or less interest. But one thing will give you joy and that is that we are going to have peace, and we shall dictate our own terms for we are now under the very walls of the City [of Mexico]. We have taken all the posts, batteries, breastworks, etc., that were thrown up from Chalco to this place; have captured some thirty or forty posts of artillery, taken many prisoners, have left from one to two thousand dead on the field. We have had some very severe fighting and we have lost many valuable officers and men; hundreds are wounded. But we have done all that we had attempted thus far and can now march into the city triumphantly. The Mexicans have at last opened their eyes and the white flag came in this morning. Commissioners have been appointed, and in all probability I shall be with you this very fall, by October or November at the furthermost. Is this not joyful?[5]

I had no idea until within a few days past what horrible sights a battlefield presented. I will give you a very brief outline of the past few days.

General Twiggs's division took the lead from Puebla, but the army concentrated at the foot of Lake Chalco and there our division, General Worth's, was in advance. We had to feel our way along very carefully as the road was on the edge of the lake, and the mountains came down almost to the road, so the enemy had every opportunity to annoy us by digging deep ditches across the road and by rolling down large rocks to fill it up. Occasionally they would fire upon us from the hills, but we reached San Agustín [on the 17th] without any loss and in fine order.

On the 18th we advanced, knowing that every inch of the ground was in a state of defense. We were about eight or nine miles from this city [Tacubaya] and two from San Antonio. We were very near the latter town when the first gun was fired. Our troops were moving very slowly. The engineers, with a squadron of dragoons to cover them, were reconnoitering in advance when the battle opened, and the first shot killed Captain Thornton of the dragoons.[6] He was sitting on his horse with his leg thrown over the pommel of his saddle and probably did not know what killed him, for it was an 18-pound shot and it literally tore him to pieces. He was buried immediately beside the road. General Worth then threw one brigade off the road and quartered it in a hacienda close by. Our brigade encamped immediately in the road where we were. We were to remain here until the engineers made a reconnaissance, and then General Scott would decide what should be done.

In the course of the afternoon [of August 18] the battery opened again. We were so near that the shells burst in our very camp. The hacienda which contained the first brigade was literally riddled with shells and round shots, but General Worth would not retreat an inch. He told the men to shelter themselves as much as they could, and not a man was hurt although [the next morning] a ball came through the room where General Worth and his staff had just eaten their breakfast, and another through a room which a portion of the troops had occupied the night before. This was on the 19th, and notwithstanding the number of shots thrown, not a man was hurt.

In the afternoon [of August 19] General Scott had formed his plans. General Pillow was to open a road [across the volcanic lava field known as the Pedregal] to San Angel, supported by General Twiggs. General Quitman was to remain at San Agustín where a depot was to be made and a hospital established. General Worth was to cover the point he then held until the batteries of San Antonio could be turned or forced. No sooner had General Pillow advanced a mile than he was attacked. General Twiggs soon came up and from 8 o'clock until dark was one continuous peal of thunder from artillery and musketry.

The fight commenced at daylight the following morning [August 20], and soon the enemy were driven from their position [at Contreras] and all the cannons taken. Probably 1,200 were left dead on the road. Our loss was severe. Lieutenants Johnstone and Easley were killed; Captains Anderson and Smith of the 2nd Infantry severely wounded; Captains Burke and Capron, and Lieutenant Hoffman of the artillery were also killed, and a great many others were so severely wounded that arms and legs have been taken off and the recovery of several is very doubtful.[7]

As soon as the enemy were in retreat we received an order from General Scott to turn the batteries in our front. Our brigade took the lead. We left the road and went about two miles over the craters of extinct volcanoes. At last we reached the main road, having passed over places that not even a mule would attempt. As soon as the enemy perceived our plans they began to dismantle their batteries as if to retreat, intending to put their guns into another fort some distance in advance [of us]. We saw them retreating and not knowing of this other battery [at the bridgehead on the Churubusco River], which was just ahead of us, charged upon the enemy. For a short time all went well, but as soon as we came under range, a most destructive fire of shot, cannister, and grape was poured upon us. The fort was flanked on the left by another which opened fire soon afterwards.[8]

For more than an hour we were exposed to this destructive fire. I saw men fall about me in every direction. Colonel Clarke was hit by a grape shot and knocked from his horse. I was standing near him and after seeing him in safety I went on with the column, but I never expected to escape unhurt. We were cut up very much before we could drive off the enemy. The 6th suffered more than any other regiment of our division. Major Bonneville, Captain Hoffman, and Lieutenants Hendrickson, Buckner, and Bacon [were wounded] and 87 others were killed and wounded. The 3rd Regiment of our brigade had 180 killed and wounded. It was a terrible fire, but the troops behaved splendidly, and the wonder is how they had courage enough to storm a fort which poured such an excessive fire upon them. But we took the batteries and immediately turned our guns upon the retreating mass.[9]

Soon the dragoons came up and we all entered into the pursuit. Hundreds of Mexicans were killed in the road. The dragoons followed up at full charge until they were brought up by a discharge from another battery [at the San Antonio Garita or gateway to Mexico City] which severely wounded three of our officers and many of our men. We had now followed up at least three miles from our starting point, stormed and taken five batteries, innumerable breastworks and musketry. Our troops were exhausted, and we encamped on the ground.

But oh, what terrible suffering, what terrible sights presented themselves on every movement. The road and its vicinity on both sides, for most of the three miles, were covered with dead and dying, bodies without heads, arms and legs, and disfigured in every horrible way! Oh, it was awful and never can I forget this day!

JOURNAL, August 23, 1847. Tacubaya.

We left Chalco on the 15th and reached San Agustín on the 17th, having had some trouble on the march by finding the road, which in many places was a narrow causeway, and sometimes for miles was on the edge of the lake and at the base of high hills. We occasionally had to send out light infantry to drive the enemy from the hills when they had a plunging fire upon us. At San Agustín we remained on the night of the 17th.

On the 18th we were under march for San Antonio, which was one league off. Captain [James L.] Mason of the Engineers, with a squadron of dragoons under Captain Thornton were reconnoitering in advance of the column, which was moving very slowly, when a battery opened its fire. . . . General Worth then ordered a reconnaissance in the neighborhood of San Antonio, and the Engineers reported the place very strongly fortified by no less than three batteries and several breastworks for infantry. We then encamped. . . .

[On August 19] General Pillow commenced operations [to open a road across the Pedregal lava field], but he had not gone far when a strong position, well fortified [at Contreras], was discovered by its opening a heavy fire. This was kept up for some hours with little loss on our side. As the enemy was in force and began to receive large reinforcements from Mexico [City], it was necessary to be energetic.

The plan was decided upon, and very early the next morning [August 20] the attack commenced, and soon our troops took all their works, many prisoners, and left hundreds dead upon the field. While this was going on, General Worth, having heard of their sucess, told us that as General Twiggs's Division had covered itself with glory, we must do something, and ordered Colonel Clarke with his brigade to advance by a flank to the rear of the batteries in front of us, take them at the point of the bayonet if we thought best, but turn them at any rate.

We started with Captain Mason of the Engineers to guide us, for he had been in the neighborhood reconnoitering. The road was very bad, all rock, covered here and there with prickly pears, the rock very uneven, here and there deep chasms, and very uneven at all times. We must have passed some three miles over this very tiresome ground. The enemy fired at us as soon as we were observed, but as the [big] guns did not have us within their range, they only fired their escopets.[10] We finally came into the road between their batteries and the city [of San Antonio]. As soon as they saw us near it, they began to retreat, evidently intending to reach the next fort in [the] rear, but as soon as we came up, the 5th Infantry was ordered to form and charge them. It did so, and for some time the fire was very severe. Many were killed and taken prisoner.

The 6th Infantry next came up and formed. The regiment was on the left of the 5th, and as we had no idea of the existence of a fourth battery, and by much the most strongly fortified, the 6th received, as it passed through the cornfields to gain the road, a shower of grape and musketry. But on the regiment went, and although at least an hour elapsed before the fort [a bridgehead on the Churbusco River] was taken, and the regiment was under the hottest fire during this period, the enemy at last gave way, and the guns of the work were turned upon them.

Duncan's battery, which was yet in rear of our brigade, opened its fire on the church of Churubusco, which flanked the fort, and poured a cross fire upon our troops. This, with one or two of the guns of the fort, which when taken were also served against it, put the enemy in and about it in motion. We immediately followed up the victory, having actually turned the town of San Antonio, which was strongly fortified by three batteries, and taken the main work at Churubusco with the point of the bayonet.

The dragoons came up soon and cut down great numbers of the flying enemy on the main road. Captain Kearny headed the charge and pushed onward until he had charged even within the walls of a sixth battery which was erected at the [San Antonio] *garita* [gateway] of the city. This battery opened its fire whilst the pursuing party were almost under the rampart and killed not only our men but even their

Charging the bridgehead at Churubusco (Richardson, *Messages and Papers of the Presidents,* 5:2147)

own retreating mass. Captain Kearny had his left arm shot off. Lieutenant Graham also was wounded by a ball in his arm, and Captain McReynolds, a third officer, was severely wounded in this charge.[11]

The Sixth Infantry suffered most in the events of the day, having lost nine killed and eighty-four wounded, many of them mortally. Our brigade lost one hundred and eighty killed and wounded, and our division three hundred and thirty-six. Colonel Clarke received a grape in his left breast, but as he was turned partially around, it did not enter the body, but it was a very severe contusion. Major Bonneville was slightly wounded, as was Captain Hoffman and Lieutenant Buckner. Lieutenants Hendrickson and Bacon were both very severely wounded in their arms. I thought for one while during the action that few of us would escape, for the round shot, grape, cannister, and musketry fell so thick, and so many dropped around me, killed or wounded, that I feared the chance of my even getting out alive was slim. But the same kind Providence, that has ever watched over me, preserved me upon this trying occasion with His invisible hand.

Many officers have been killed and others severely cut to pieces. Captains Burke and Capron, and Lieutenants Johnstone and Hoffman of the 1st Artillery were killed, and Irons and Martin severely wounded.[12] In the 2nd Infantry, Captain Anderson and Lieutenant Easley were killed, and Captain Smith badly wounded. Many more, whose names I do not now recollect, have been killed and wounded. But my kind Parent has spared me to enjoy many happy years I trust with my own dearest Kate.

Among the prisoners taken were between 80 and 90 deserters from our own army.[13] I find some eight or ten from the 6th Infantry. An exchange has been made of prisoners. The Mexicans had about 200 Americans, taken at different times. All who were taken in the north were sent to the capital and paraded before the people. We took in the last battles upwards of two thousand prisoners, seven generals, and a hundred officers of lower grades.

As we rode into town [Tacubaya] yesterday, I observed a monument beside the road with this inscription: "This road was constructed by the Texan prisoners under General Santa Anna." It is a fine, hard, macadamized road, but the Yankees could not stand the inscription, for I noticed that the fragments of it were lying scattered in any direction this morning. Some, perhaps, of the very men who worked on the road, turned out in the night and destroyed it.[14]

LETTER, August 23, 1847. Tacubaya.

I learned this morning that there is an armistice, and we are to be put in possession of all the remaining works in the neighborhood of the city. Peace has been conquered. I have never lost my sanguine belief during the fight that I should be unharmed. I learned that Captain Anderson of the 2nd Infantry is dead, and probably several more will die of their wounds.

I cannot begin to relate the many brilliant achievements of the two days during which there was hardly a cessation of cannonading. But you will read in the papers pretty much all, and when I get home, I will have enough that will not appear in any paper. One thing I must tell you: we took a large number of prisoners who were deserters from our own ranks. They were very active in the fight [at Churubusco] and killed many of our own men, but a court-martial is now in session, and I presume they will all be hung, for shooting is too good for them. One of them was a major [in the Mexican army] named Riley. He deserted from the 5th Infantry and had charge of a gun at Monterrey and Buena Vista. He will be hung higher than the rest.[15]

This [Tacubaya] is a beautiful village where many of the people of the city have their country houses, and most of the foreign ministers and consuls reside here. We may, although it is doubtful, remain here until we can hear from Washington. I understand the terms of the treaty have already been decided upon, and as a matter of course it must be such as we wish, for we have the [Mexican] nation in our hands. General Scott has his headquarters here and General Worth is here with his division. General Twiggs is at San Angel.

I hope we shall soon be able to have a regular mail established between this city and Veracruz. I would give the world to hear from you.

I cannot be too thankful to Providence that I am in perfect health. I have seen those around me fall, but I have been protected by the Invisible Hand. I have carried your daguerreotype in my pocket and had I been shot, I would have had the consolation of having it in my last moments. But I hope I shall be able to join you [soon].

I have been wondering whether it would be better for me to get a furlough as soon as the war is over and go to New England to visit my parents and sisters; or whether it would be best for me to get a short leave and go to Alton, and then after a few months get a long leave and go East. Of course everybody will be trying to get a leave or furlough as soon as we get home.

I listened today to a whole pile of [Mexican] letters intercepted the day after the battle. They were in the mail carried out of the city. From them it appears that the enemy had 32,000 soldiers and we had but 7,000; and yet such a threshing they got! I considered the [Mexican artillery] batteries that formed the line from San Antonio to Churubusco impregnable, but all was taken at the point of the bayonet. You have no idea what our army, small as it is, can do. Having been successful thus far, nothing can stop them, and although hundreds were shot down around the others, the cry was "Onward," and with a cheer they would rush to the cannon's mouth.

One [Mexican] writer, speaking of the army, says, "We trusted for safety to our numbers, but our enemy sleeps not and knows no fear." He must have been connected with the army, for he spoke the truth, and from the time we left Chalco we kept our eyes open, I assure you. The night of the 19th, after the battle had been opened, while the enemy was sleeping in security of numbers and choice of position, our little army was busy all night, although it rained in torrents, in putting troops across ravines and over rocks that were deemed impassable by the enemy, and at the very dawn of the day we were ready to charge from all sides. But the charging is over, and I trust we shall soon be on our way home.

Do not forget to let me know, in your next letter, whether you get the money I send you.

When the official reports of the battles are published, look for General Worth's, Colonel Clarke's, and Colonel McIntosh's [units], and you will see what our brigade, and particularly our regiment, the 6th, did.[16]

Farewell. God bless you.

Your affectionate husband.

JOURNAL, August 29, 1847. Tacubaya.

I attended church this afternoon at General Scott's headquarters at the archbishop's palace [in Tacubaya]. There were quite a number of foreigners, residents of this place, who attended, besides a room full of our own officers. Of those absent who usually attend were three, who when we last met at the Lord's table were present, but now their places were vacant. One, Captain [Charles] Hanson of the 7th Infantry, was killed on the 20th. Captain [Joseph R.] Smith of the 2nd Infantry is very severely wounded, and Lieutenant Martin, 2nd [First] Artillery, has lost an arm. Next Sunday will be the first Sunday of the month, and I trust we shall be blessed with the privileges of the day [Communion].

I visited this morning the garden of the German consul [Frederick Gerolt]. It was a beautiful spot. I cannot enumerate the hundreds of fruits and flowers which I saw there, but among the former were apples, pears, peaches, plums, apricots, quinces, pomegranates, figs, cherries, English walnuts, strawberries, grapes, oranges, lemons, limes, olives, etc. And of flowers, there were dahlias, roses, pinks, verbena, passion flowers, sweet peas, and I know not how many whose names I knew not. And there were some beautiful shade trees, some that I never before saw.

JOURNAL, August 31, 1847. Tacubaya.

I have been engaged today in mustering and inspecting the three regiments composing the 2nd Brigade, 1st Division, and a hard day's work

I have had of it. I began with the 5th Infantry at 8 o'clock, finished by half past 10, then went and before dinner had completed the 6th, having visited both hospitals, guardhouses, etc. At 2 o'clock I went to the 8th [Infantry], and it was nearly night before I completed my labours.

I was told today by Captain [Benjamin] Huger of the Ordnance Department that we captured in the late actions 300 rounds of musket cartridges per man for an army of 30,000 men. These cartridges were made of the best materials, the powder being a very hard grain, probably English manufacture.

JOURNAL, September 1, 1847. Tacubaya.

I have been busy today examining muster rolls, and have finished only those of our regiment [6th Infantry] and the 5th Infantry. Today is the first day of autumn. How differently I am employed now from what I was last year at this time.

JOURNAL, September 6, 1847. Tacubaya.

Yesterday by the kindness of Him who has ever blessed me, smiling upon me at all times, I was permitted to kneel at the Lord's table and partake of the holy sacrament. It was an interesting occasion, and oh when, when shall I enjoy this blessed privilege with my beloved Kate by my side? God only knows.

Yesterday and even today we were all looking forward to the time when we should be on our way home, but tonight our hopes are dissipated, and we are as far from peace as we were on the 20th. The armistice has been formally broken, and after 48 hours, hostilities begin again. It is all for the best, for an all wise Providence overrules all for our good, and we must not murmur. But if we do have to fight, the Mexicans will wish they had never given us cause to begin to act on the offensive, for all, or nearly all, are of opinion that we should have gone into Mexico [City] on the 20th or 21st. And if we have to fight our way in, the carnage will be dreadful; the soldiers will not be restrained, and we shall see sights — those of us who are fortunate enough to get in — which will be revolting. May God in his providence yet cause this people to act for their own good.

LETTER, September 6, 1847. Tacubaya.

I do not know when I shall have an opportunity to send this. I have now several letters written within the past month, but as no mail has left within so long a time I hope one will start soon for Veracruz. I feel homesick, for I cannot hear from you. Your last letter was written the 23rd of June.

I began to write this morning, and since then we are notified that the armistice is broken, notice having been given by General Scott, and in 48 hours hostilities will begin again. I trust they will not be of long duration, although we must fight and be victorious without a doubt. Still I hope we shall not lose any more of our brave army. We are much better prepared to be victorious now than when we left Puebla, and we have a much heavier siege train. Our men have gained experience in the late battles, and the Mexicans have lost what little morale they possessed. A few days will decide, and I shall lay this letter aside for a few days.

JOURNAL, September 8, 1847. Tacubaya.

This day has been a sad one to many of us, for we have seen some of our best, our bravest officers and men shot down around us. We formed our division at 3 o'clock in the morning for the purpose of attacking the enemy, whose line extended from the fort [Castle] of Chapultepec about a mile to the southwest, and rested on a hacienda [named Morales]. There was a foundry [El Molino del Rey] near the left of their line, which was to be taken, as it was believed to contain several pieces of artillery which were being finished, bells having been carried out of the city within a few days past to use in casting them. A party composed of 500 men, the veterans of the division, was chosen for the storming party. Major Wright was to have command. Colonel Garland's brigade was to go to the right of this party and obtain a lodgement in a cypress grove under Chapultepec. Our brigade was to move to the left and support the storming party, if required, or which was more probable, to attack the center of the enemy's right wing, cut him in two and cut up the portion thus severed from the main body. [17]

Colonel Clarke, being still sore from his late wound, was unable to take command, consequently Lieutenant Burwell and myself re-

Battle of Molino del Rey (Anderson, *An Artillery Officer in the Mexican War,* p. 310)

ported in person to Colonel McIntosh, as his staff. The night was cloudy and we did not get our position until nearly dawn of day. We advanced down a gentle slope, about two hundred yards; here, as we were advancing in line, when within about seventy yards of the enemy's line of breastworks, we were received by a very severe fire of musketry. This, with occasional rounds of grape, cut us up considerably, but still no one thought of retreating. On the brigade went, but the enemy was in such force that the fire was continuous, like the roll of drums. Our men could not stand it and gave way. It was just before this that I saw poor Burwell fall. He was shot just above the knee. I turned toward him, but saw that he was not dangerously wounded, and went on in the charge. We were driven back; again the troops rallied and attempted to reach the enemy's position, but the fire was so murderous that the men again fell back. And it was only when Colonel Duncan's battery opened a fire of grape that they were driven out.

Then I returned to look for my companion, but he was dead. He lay just where he had fallen, his leg had been broken just above the knee. When we were driven back, some [Mexican] lancers had galloped up and one of them had laid open his skull to the brain for four or five inches. After that, some other devil had sneaked up and before robbing him, for fear that he might be alive, had stabbed him three times with a bayonet, and then rifled his pockets, taking his ring from his finger and his sword from his body. The fiend even had commenced stripping his body of his clothes but had not time to finish his hellish design. When I found him, his favorite pointer dog was lying nesting close beside him, licking his face, but like his master, he had been shot and died in a few moments. I picked up from the ground a lock of my friend's hair which had been severed from his head by the murderous lance which killed him. I had him taken and laid beside three other officers of his own regiment who had likewise fallen, having died like heroes: Colonel Scott, Captain Merrill, and Lieutenant Strong. [18]

Our loss was terrible, being 339 killed, wounded and missing— only nine of the missing, and they were without doubt among the killed. Among forty officers in our brigade, but twenty escaped; twenty were killed or wounded. Colonel McIntosh was shot through the thigh and fell; whilst lying on the ground, he received another ball below the knee which passed up his leg under the muscles and lodged in his groin. As the line fell back, he was dragged off by two men, or he would have met the fate of his aide. I wonder how any one escaped under the severe fire to which we were exposed. [19]

After the works were taken, Lieutenant Armstrong was engaged in removing ammunition from a magazine. When he had taken several loads, he attempted to blow up the building, but, poor fellow, he was covered with the ruins and killed. [20]

Captains Walker and Cady and Lieutenant Ernst were wounded. Ernst will lose his right arm. Walker was shot through the body, and although a very severe wound, he will probably get well. Captain Ayers was killed, also Lieutenant Farry of the artillery. [21]

We captured seven pieces of artillery and took seven hundred and fifty prisoners, fifty being commissioned officers. The enemy's loss in killed was very severe, being without doubt treble ours, but their force was at least ten times our own. It was a dearly-bought victory on our side. We gained all we attempted, but oh we shall think of the cost as long as we live.

LETTER, September 8, 1847. Tacubaya.

My Beloved Wife:

Sad and melancholy are the events of this day [the Battle of Molino del Rey]. Many of our best officers and men have been cut to pieces. I cannot give any particulars. We were up all last night, and at 3 o'clock this morning took position opposite the enemy's line, to attack at the dawn of day. But, unfortunately, we were not sufficiently acquainted with the position occupied by the enemy, and in driving thousands of the rascals from behind walls and breastworks, have suffered far more than in the battles of San Antonio and Churubusco. Colonel Clarke, from his wound, was unable to take command of the brigade, and Lieutenant Burwell and myself reported to Colonel McIntosh, who is next in command, as his staff officers. Poor Burwell was shot by my side. Colonel McIntosh was badly shot, but he may recover. A kind Providence has again brought me through a thousand dangers to which I was exposed. It was awful! Words cannot express the murderous fire to which we were exposed, and I will not attempt to describe the sickening sights of this unfortunate day. I say "unfortunate," for although we drove the enemy from their position and occupy their works, still it was a dearly-bought victory and one which will be remembered by all engaged.

I feel very lonely tonight, I assure you, with my roommate and companion dead, and I sit here alone. We started out this morning together; we were charging the enemy's works and he was shot. I saw him fall, but I could not halt for it was necessary for all, particularly the officers, to rush on. We were repulsed; again we charged, and again were driven back. After the enemy was routed, I returned to look for poor Burwell, and there he lay, just as he had fallen. Burwell was a generous, noble, and brave fellow.

Other officers have fallen, and a great number too. I believe the 6th Regiment suffered comparatively less than the 5th and 8th.

JOURNAL, September 9, 1847. Tacubaya.

We buried today the officers and soldiers who fell in the murderous affair of yesterday. One hundred and seventeen poor but gallant fellows lie side by side in a field on the side hill in rear of the bishop's palace and in sight of the battlefield. Mr. McCarty performed the service over them, and not an eye was dry, for we had all of us lost those whom we loved. They were buried with military honors, and I trust their memories will remain fresh in the hearts of those of us who knew them and witnessed their gallantry upon this as well as other occasions.

Oh, how shall I express my gratitude to my Heavenly Father for having brought me unharmed out of this terrible battle. Whilst hundreds were shot down, and I had not, I fully believed at the time, one chance in fifty of escaping the same fate, my Holy Father shielded me, and I am yet in the land of the living. May I by my future conduct express my thankfulness more than I can by words.

None but an eyewitness can realize the scenes which were presented at the hospital where the wounded lay at the close of the action, bodies shot in every part, limbs terribly mangled by fragments of shells and round shot. Most of the wounded, however, were hit by bullets.

LETTER, September 9, 1847. Tacubaya.

I have just returned from the funeral ceremonies of 117 officers and men who were buried together. Poor but brave men who deserved a better fate!

Tomorrow morning twenty deserters who formed against us at Churubusco will be hanged, and some forty more will probably be, for they were caught at the same time. Their sentence has not yet been published.

We have been very busy moving our siege train today, and about Sunday, the 12th, we shall be in the city. I hear that the Mexican loss on the 8th was very severe: nearly 3,000 killed or wounded, including two generals, León and Balderas, and some 700 prisoners, including 50 officers. Our loss was upwards of 600. I suppose not more than one-fourth are killed, but many of those must die, and a great proportion of the others will be crippled or maimed for life.[22]

JOURNAL, September 10, 1847. Tacubaya.

Today Captain Huger has been moving the siege train out of town [Tacubaya], and I understand has now thirty heavy pieces planted. I suppose tomorrow or next day the firing will be opened upon the City [of Mexico].

This morning the sentences of some of our deserters were published. These men [the San Patricios or St. Patrick's] were found fighting in the enemy's ranks, and out of twenty-nine tried by the court of which Colonel Riley was president, twenty were hanged. The remaining nine were branded on a cheek with the letter D and received 50 lashes on the bare back.[23]

JOURNAL, September 11, 1847. Tacubaya.

Lieutenant Burbank died yesterday, and we followed him to the grave today. He was shot in the left side, and I thought the wound was not dangerous, for I saw him on the battlefield and he was cheerful and said he suffered very little pain. But he too has gone with many other gallant fellows. Today Captain E. K. Smith has also died from his wound; he was shot through the head and there was little hope that he could recover. He is the fifth officer of this [Fifth] regiment who is gone within the past 3 days—four killed on the ground: Colonel Scott, Captain Merrill, Lieutenants Strong and Burwell.[24]

The enemy made some demonstrations this afternoon. We went out with a squadron of dragoons and the 8th Infantry, but after some little skirmishing, the enemy, which was only a large body of cavalry, retreated, and we returned quietly to our quarters.

JOURNAL, September 12, 1847. Tacubaya.

Sunday. This day has been occupied in opening our batteries upon Chapultepec. The effect has been to destroy in some measure their works. The main work seems to be pretty well riddled. Still, we have not yet silenced their batteries which fire at intervals at us. General Twiggs opened at the lower part of the city and silenced one of their batteries there, but I judge we have not yet gained much.[25]

Oh when shall we conquer and have Sunday to spend as a day of rest! I trust after we do get possession of the city we shall not be called out on this day. What is my poor wife doing today? God bless her! and restore her to me in his own good time. Last Sunday Captain Merrill joined with us at the holy communion table; now he lies in his grave, having died waving his sword over his head. How many more of our brave officers and soldiers shall we lose before we are conquerors of this miserable race, God only knows; but I hope and pray not many.

JOURNAL, September 13, 1847. Mexico City.

A storming party [for Chapultepec Castle] was detailed last night, and this morning our division was under arms at 5 o'clock to go to the Molino del Rey and be ready to assist the storming party. We marched out of Tacubaya, and as we came within range of the guns of Chapultepec, they opened upon us, and before we could get shelter under the walls of the houses, a great many shells and round shot were thrown among us. However, we fortunately escaped with little loss. We remained here perhaps half an hour, when we received orders for Colonel Clarke's brigade to go and support the stormers. So on we went at a full run, and in passing through a large cypress grove at the foot of the hill upon which the fortress is built, we received a sweeping fire of grape and musketry. But as soon as we reached the base of the hill, we were safe from all artillery, as the depression was too great. We found the storming party had reached the ditch which surrounds the fort, and although our men had received a pretty severe fire, many officers and men having been killed and wounded, still there was no foothold in the work, not even the ladders for scaling had come up. But in about half an hour the brave command began to divest the cowards, and soon the stars and stripes were waving over the fortress. Our brigade in reality formed a large part of the storming party.

We took a great many prisoners, among them General [Nicolás] Bravo. We found a great many mines about the work, and long leather hoses communicating with them outside, [designed] to have blown us sky high after we took possession. But the rascals had not even courage to fire the train.[26]

But we reformed in the course of an hour, after General Scott had come up from Tacubaya and had been cheered and given us a speech. I must mention one sentiment which was given, and which received three times three [cheers]: "Our wives, children, and sweethearts."

We soon were on the road to the city; it runs in almost a right line for more than a mile. Just at the suburbs there was a battery, and all the housetops were lined with [Mexican] infantry. As we came near, we received a volley, and it was kept up some fifteen minutes, when by flanking them, we drove them [back].

Storming of Chapultepec castle (William H. Bartlett, *The History of the United States of North America*, 3 vols. [New York, 1856], frontispiece, vol. 2)

We were now at the entrance of San Cosme, a street which runs all the way to the main plaza of the city. We advanced up the street and had not gone more than two squares when another battery opened upon us, and the housetops seemed to be alive with sharpshooters. So we left the street, took to the houses on either side, and [with pickaxes] picked our way through from house to house. We had also a section of the mountain howitzer battery, which we carried to the tops of the houses, and by throwing shells over onto the houses ahead of us, cleared the way and soon came to battery number two. We took to the road again, but soon found another battery still ahead of us. Again we entered the houses, and with pick and crowbar, worked our way. We had to work hard, for it was near night, and General Worth said we should not sleep until we had taken that battery. And it was not until quite dark when we had reached within thirty yards of the enemy and opened our fire, when the cowards again ran. We turned a large iron gun upon them and gave them a few rounds.

We were now inside the city; we were hungry and tired, yet we were not through. Colonel Garland quartered his brigade at the Garita [the gateway of San Cosme], but our brigade went on as far as we could, for grape and bullets were continually showering down the street. We, however, crept along a couple of squares and quartered the 5th and 6th on the right hand side and the 8th on the left of the street. General Worth now ordered Captain Hagner to throw a bomb occasionally over towards the center of the city; this was kept up at intervals until about midnight.[27]

JOURNAL, September 14, 1847. Mexico City.

I could not sleep, for the excitement of the day [yesterday] had kept me up during almost ceaseless exertion from daylight. About two o'clock in the morning we heard a horn coming blasting down the street. I went out and, behold, there stood Mr. [Riva] Palacio, who said Santa Anna and his army had vamoosed, and two commissioners had come out to turn over the city to General Scott on any terms. I went down with him to General Worth, who sent them on to General Scott.[28]

We were up at dawn of day and moved up towards the [National] Palace, but soon we were fired upon by persons from the tops of the houses, and it took us all day to get the city quiet. But at night all was still, and we retired to our beds, glad to get some sleep.

CHAPTER FOUR

Occupation of Mexico's Capital

♣

LETTER, September 15, 1847. Mexico City.

My Dear Wife:

How shall I express my gratitude for being permitted to write again? Kind Heaven has surely sent a guardian angel to protect me, for while so many have fallen on the battlefield, I have again come out unharmed.

On the 12th we opened a fire from three batteries upon the fortress [Chapultepec] which lay to the west of the city. The fire was continued all day and to good purpose. That night a party was detailed to storm the castle. It was a desperate undertaking, but it had to be done.

General Worth formed his division at 3 o'clock in the morning [of September 13], and we moved very slowly to support the storming party. As we crossed the plain, within a few hundred yards of the fort, a heavy fire of shells and grapeshot was opened upon us, but we fortunately lost but few men before we got under cover of an old stone wall. Soon we advanced. Well, up the hill we went and found the storming party; our coming up gave fresh courage, and soon we poured out fire on all sides, and in five minutes the stars and stripes floated over Chapultepec. It was a glorious sight.[1] We took many prisoners, but again we lost some officers and men.

After getting a little breath we were ordered forward to go into Mexico City that night. General Worth's division had the honor of going ahead. It is a mile from the fort [of Chapultepec] to the [Santo Tomás] suburb of the city. We got there without any resistance, but here we were greeted by showers of grape and musketry, for a battery was established there. We soon drove them off. The [Mexican] artillery withdrew some four or five squares where a battery had been erected. The [roofs of the] houses were all lined with their infantry, but we left the streets and entered the houses on both sides and commenced making our way toward the Palace by going from house to house [by pickaxe]. We worked hard, I can assure you. When we

65

reached the battery, we found it had been withdrawn again and was placed this time just in the [San Cosme] garita of the city.

It was nearly dark but we pushed on and got within thirty yards of the battery. It was almost dark when we presented ourselves, and not more than a hundred or two at that, when again they fled and in such haste that we captured their artillery. It was a grand sight. I should think there were some 3,000 or 4,000 of the rascals. We turned the pieces on the retreating mass and gave them what they had been giving us for an hour or two previously.

It was now 8 o'clock [on the 13th], and we were in the city. We were perfectly exhausted and yet in such a position that it was necessary for us to be on the q.v., for still another battery had opened up the street. We, however, got into the houses again and we would throw a few shells over toward the center of the city. This was done at intervals until about midnight when two commissioners came down and said the city surrendered on our own terms, and that Santa Anna had again withdrawn all his troops and what artillery he had left.

The next morning we moved up toward the Palace, but vagabonds began to fire at us from roofs of the houses. We immediately took to the house tops again and silenced the cowards. We are now in the center of the capital, and our flag flies over the National Palace, but the Mexican Army has gone and the government also.[2] What we are able to do now I do not know. I am sure we have fought enough, and they must feel convinced that we can whip them, small as our army is. But how I long to see you and tell you of the thousand incidents which have occurred since I left. I cannot write in a week what I can tell you in an hour.

I captured a fine horse, saddle, and bridle on the 13th. I was with the storming party when it entered Fort Chapultepec, and there I selected him from a stable full of horses which belonged to the officers who were killed or taken prisoners. My horse belonged to a colonel of the 6th Lancers.

I must tell you how nearly Santa Anna came being taken a prisoner. He was actually let down out of the window by a rope on the side opposite where we entered. I wish we had caught him. We got General Bravo, however, and hundreds of others [Mexican soldiers]. But I cannot speak of success without calling to mind the brave fellows who lost their lives while fighting so valiantly. And I escaped without even a scratch. I have been so near those being shot that their

Scott's entrance into Mexico City (Edward D. Mansfield, *The Mexican War: A History of Its Origins* [New York, 1848], frontispiece)

blood would fly all over me. The nearest shot that I have yet received was on the 8th in charging the enemy's line at Molino del Rey. I had reached a ditch through which we had driven the enemy's infantry. Here we were under partial fire from their battery. I had taken a musket from a soldier who was wounded, and I had fired half a dozen times when an escopette bullet just grazed my fingers, skinning them. Half an inch lower would have taken them all off, but I escaped even that loss while so many have lost their limbs.

I have just learned that [First] Lieutenant [Charles F.] Morris of the 8th Infantry, who lost his leg on that day, is dead. Almost all who have had their limbs amputated have died afterwards.

I am tired of thinking and writing about these bloody actions, and I sincerely pray that I shall not have to go into any more. A person can get accustomed to anything so as to be indifferent to the most revolting sights, but I trust I shall have witnessed all that I shall have to. Your daguerreotype has afforded me much consolation in all these times. Captain Walker of our regiment was severely wounded. He had his wife's miniature in his pocket and a bullet struck it.

I have met a little boy here who is a great pet of mine. He is only twelve years old, yet he speaks fluently English, Spanish, and French. He calls me Don Rodolfo [Sir Ralph].

JOURNAL, September 21, 1847. Mexico City.

We have now been in the city a week, and it is growing daily more
quiet, although hardly a day passes without one or more of our soldiers being assassinated. They get intoxicated and wander into bye
streets and almost invariably are stabbed. We hear rumors of the in-
troduction of a large body of armed men into the city, who are to
rise and overpower the guards, murder us all, etcetera. But a cow-
ardly race who cannot defend its capital will never do this.

JOURNAL, September 23, 1847. Mexico City.

I have been confined to my bed for the past four days with a bilious
attack besides a severe diarrhea. But I am well enough today to attend
to my usual duties. I attended this afternoon the funeral of Lieutenant Ernst of my Regiment. Poor fellow, he was wounded on the 8th
in the battle of the Molino del Rey, and was not considered dangerous
until a day or two since. But he died last night and was buried in the
[cemetery of the] convent of San Fernando, [established by] an order
of friars, with the usual Roman Catholic ceremonies.

JOURNAL, September 25, 1847. Mexico City.

I went this morning with Mr. Hill, a Georgian who was taken prisoner at Mier some years ago, and who has been under Santa Anna's
charge here since, and with Mr. Baygally, an English gentleman, and
visited the [Art] Academy of San Carlos.[3] This is an institution established a long time ago [in 1785] by Charles III of Spain, and which,
after having been neglected many years, has been within two or three
[years] revived by the Mexican government and is now a credit to the
nation. The galleries of paintings, statuary, etc., are good. Some of
the former are by old masters, and some are the work of young Mexicans which do them much credit.

   We also visited the [National] Museum where there are a great
many of the old idols, and the great stone which is so celebrated as
the [Aztec] sacrificial stone. Here also is the beautiful and magnificent bronze statute of Carlos Quarto; it was designed and cast by two
Mexicans, and is, I believe, the third in point of superiority in the
world.[4] In the market also I saw the statue of General Santa Anna,

which is a fine piece of statuary. The calendar of Montezuma, which is a large stone of some ten feet in diameter, is one of the wonders of the world, and is worked into the side of the grand cathedral [of Mexico City].

JOURNAL, September 26, 1847. Mexico City.

I attended church this afternoon in the [National] Palace. Mr. McCarty preached. Text: "God is love." The house was full; besides more than the usual number of officers, there were a great number of the foreign residents of this place. It was gratifying to meet once more after recent events and offer up our prayers and praises to our Heavenly Father. Next Sunday Mr. McCarty proposes to preach a thanksgiving sermon in commemoration of our late victories, and in the morning we are again to be blessed with the privilege of partaking of the holy sacrament.

LETTER, September 26, 1847. Mexico City.

My Dear Wife:

I am beginning to lose all patience, as the mails come and go and no letters from you. I am very well and hope and pray that you are; but it is hard to hear nothing from you. Still, "Hope on; hope ever," and all will yet be well.

I attended the funeral of Lieutenant Ernst on Thursday. He was wounded in the battle of Molino del Rey on the 8th, and he died of his wounds. He was to have been married as soon as he could get a leave. Colonel McIntosh, I think, will die in a short time; he is severely wounded. And hundreds of others, wounded in different battles between the 20th of August and the 13th of September, will die, and daily some dozens of men are carried to their long home.

I had an attack of fever on Sunday last. I had two doctors. I am now well. I was exposed the night we got into the city, sleeping without even a blanket, and took cold. I am now in comfortable quarters and shall be as long as we remain here.

During the armistice [August 23 to September 7] many wrote letters to send under safety guard from Santa Anna. General Scott sent them with his official communications into the city, and that rascal Santa Anna, in violence of all honor and strictly against the articles of the armistice, gets his clique around him in his palace and then breaks open all the papers and had a laugh at our expense. But we laugh at them now. We will soon have open communication from here to Veracruz, and then we can get all letters regularly.

JOURNAL, September 27, 1847. Mexico City.

We hear today that Santa Anna, when he left this city, went back to Puebla and attacked [the American garrison and hospital commanded by] Colonel Childs. But as he [Childs] was reinforced the day before by an arrival of a detachment of troops from Veracruz, he was able to give him a pretty severe thrashing.

JOURNAL, September 28, 1847. Mexico City.

I attended today the funeral of Colonel McIntosh. He was severely wounded on the 8th at the battle of El Molino del Rey and died from his wounds night before last. He was buried in the English burial ground, and a braver man than Colonel McIntosh never lived. I had him carried off the field after he was wounded, and he was continually asking, "Is that fort taken yet?" This was the work where we were repulsed in attempting to carry it. He was wounded in charging, and as the men fell back, they brought off the colonel, and he would not leave the field until the work was taken.

JOURNAL, October 2, 1847. Mexico City.

We had a genuine earthquake this morning. I was standing, leaning over a table reading, feeling, as I thought, suddenly very dizzy. Everything seemed to reel, but I soon found the walls of the house cracking, and on looking out into the streets, I perceived all the Mexicans on their knees, calling on the saints for protection. The aqueduct was broken in fifty places, the fountains were half emptied of their water, and nearly every house shows evidence of having been shaken from its foundation. The sensation produced upon me was very disagreeable, and I have no curiosity to experience another. But I am told that during this month we may expect them at any time.

LETTER, October 2, 1847. Mexico City.

My Dear Wife:

We have now seen the last of Mexican curiosities, for this morning we had an earthquake, and it was no laughing matter, I assure you. It made me sick, so sick that I did not get entirely over it for an hour or two. The effect was precisely like the rocking of a ship. The earth trembled and the houses were, I thought, in danger of tumbling over us on all sides. The earth opened in several places and closed again, throwing out with great violence the water which ran in. I have no wish to experience any more, for although we can whip the Mexicans, the earthquakes are too hard for us.

I have been able to collect some curiosities and have bought you a present or two. I went shopping a few days ago with an acquaintance of mine, and selected a shawl for you. She says it is a beautiful one, but you can judge when you see it.[5]

Colonel McIntosh died some days ago. Only think of it, Lieutenant Burwell and I were his aides on the 8th. They both are now dead, while I escaped. Generals Twiggs's and Worth's divisions have lost one hundred officers killed or wounded.

The [Mexican] Congress meets in a few days, and we hope peace will be established. Oh, how glad I shall be for I am tired of fighting! We can whip these Mexicans in any numbers, but they are not worth whipping at such expense. The brave fellows that we have lost are worth more than the whole Mexican nation. General Scott thinks, in fact there is a general opinion, that we will never meet the Mexican army in any force again. So you need not be in any uneasiness about me. I am in perfect health. Everyone remarks on how well I look.

It is almost six months now since we parted. Soon it will be the anniversary of our wedding day.

Ever your loving husband.

JOURNAL, October 3, 1847. Mexico City.

Sunday. I attended church this afternoon. Mr. McCarty preached a thanksgiving sermon in honor of our late victories. Text: I Samuel, [chapter] 12, [verse] 24, "Only fear the Lord, and serve him with truth, with all your heart; for consider how great things he hath done for you." Although it is the first Sunday in the month, we did not have communion this morning, but Mr. McCarty is to administer it next Sunday. The sermon today was excellent, and the officers were so much pleased with it that a copy has been called for, to have it printed.

JOURNAL, October 14, 1847. Mexico City.

I attended this morning the funeral of Lieutenant Bacon, Lieutenent Shackelford, and Dr. Roberts. All died of their wounds. We have been expecting for more than a week past that they must die, for they have been wasting away gradually, and now, poor fellows, they lie side by side in the English burying ground on San Cosme. Captain Walker is very low from his wounds, and I am fearful he is in a very critical state. [He survived.][6]

JOURNAL, October 20, 1847. Mexico City.

Today is the anniversary of my marriage — the first one. One year ago today I was blessed with the hand of her who was my choice of all my female acquaintances, being better calculated to make me happy and to be to me all that a wife should be. One year has passed away, and during this time, I have been absent from her upwards of one half of it! And until yesterday I had not heard a word from her for more than three months! But yesterday a letter from her, brought up by the British courier, reached me, and it was indeed a treasure. My poor Kate, writing that she has not heard from me since early in June, and all the papers have been filled with incorrect stories of battles, etc., and her mind has been constantly agitated by hope and fear.

"Heavenly Father, the protector of all that trust in Thee, grant to my beloved wife health of body and cheerfulness of spirits. Defend and guard her in my absence with thy tenderest care. Thou knowst all her joys and sorrows, her hopes and her fears, let thy blessings be on her head night and day; support her in all her necessities, strengthen her in all her temptations, comfort her in all her sorrows, guide her in all the changes the chances of this mortal life, and in thine own due time may we be blessed in each others embrace."

This year just closed has been one filled with interesting events to me, events which will be remembered during life. The first part of the year I spent at home with my dear Kate. We were perfectly happy, and sad was our separation; for happy as we were on our wedding day, every day as long as we were together seemed to add to our joys. But the day of separation came at last, and we were torn asunder. For upwards of six months have we been separated.

I have been engaged in my profession, have passed through five battles: San Antonio, Churubusco, El Molino del Rey, Chapultepec, and San Cosme. These have been hard contested fights, as the loss will show. We left Puebla with 10,638 rank and file, and of this number in the Valley of Mexico three thousand have fallen — killed or wounded. Of the officers, 383 are killed or wounded. Then how great ought my gratitude be to Him who has kindly guarded me in all this danger, and permitted me to have hope of yet meeting her whom I love, whilst so many have left their wives and children to mourn their loss. God grant that I may, as long as I live, express my gratitude for these mercies, and when the next anniversary of my marriage rolls round, may I be blessed with the presence of my beloved wife.

LETTER, October 20, 1847. Mexico City.

My Dear Kate:

Just think, we have been married a whole year today! Just think how swiftly the time has flown and how many important events are crowded within its limits!

I put a check for $150.00 in the last letter I wrote you, but that letter has not gone, so you will probably get all the $300.00 I sent at once. I have been saving as I could, but everything in this country costs more than it does in the United States. Tea is $5.00 a pound, and many other things in proportion.

General Worth, I understand, has applied to be sent with his division to garrison the district of Jalapa. I hope he will be sent, for we then can at least hear from each other oftener. I am tired of seeing the distress and misery that is to be witnessed every day in this country. I think I shall better appreciate my beloved country if ever I get into it again.

I am so proud of my horse Rock; he has been of the greatest service to me, and there are two beautiful rides in this country. The Alameda is one. This is a fine, large grove of poplar trees almost in the heart of the city; there are beautiful fountains, birds, and flowers there. The other is the Paseo, which is a road on the outskirts of the city where everybody rides in the afternoon. There are some beautiful fountains there, too, but the recent earthquake has stopped the water from playing.

They have got our Major Bonneville up before the court-martial [board] for misbehavior before the enemy. It is a hard case, but from all the reputation he had gained from his Rocky Mountain experience, he certainly did not lead our regiment in the late actions.[7] In two cases he gave the order to charge but forgot to follow. I do wish Colonel Loomis had been here. He would have given us more eclat; then we would have gained. But perhaps we have gotten glory enough. I am satisfied.

Lieutenant Bacon's death promotes Flint to be first lieutenant. Lieutenant Nelson is now at the head of the [promotion] list, and I am next. But I hope, although there is no telling with any degree of certainty, that I shall get a brevet when Congress meets. But I must be content and take promotion as it comes.[8]

Major Woods is stationed with his regiment at the Fortress of Chapultepec. He comes over and dines with me occasionally. Of course I have much to say to him about you, as he saw you so much later than anyone else here.[9]

The climate here is perfectly delightful. It is sufficiently cool to wear flannels and yet not too cold. I am quartered in the house of a Colonel Mariano Deocamentes, an old Spaniard, who pets me very much and calls me his son. He has a fine house with a beautiful court-yard full of flowers and fountains and a large aviary. I should think there are one hundred birds in it, and much sweet music as they keep up! The house is near one of the public streets leading from the palace, and it is full of people all the day long. There is as much passing as in either the Astor [Hotel] in New York or the St. Charles [Hotel] in New Orleans. Every morning I go out guard-mounting in the Alameda and turn off the division guards.

Well, I must bid you goodbye. I think I shall soon have an opportunity to send letters by a regular mail which will start in the course of ten days.

We have rumors that as soon as General Scott can hear from Washington we are to be withdrawn, but it is difficult to look into the future. It is hard for me to be separated from you. It is going on four months since I heard anything from you.

God bless you, is the daily prayer of your truly affectionate husband.

LETTER, October 25, 1847. Mexico City.

My Beloved Kate:

General Scott has decided, at last, to send off a train [to Veracruz], the first one since June 4th. Of course I profit by the opportunity. How thankful I was to get a letter from you last week. It was dated September 7th and was Number 24. The last previous to this is Number 13. So you see about a dozen of your letters have been lost. I may get them, though, in a train which is now at Puebla. In your letter you say you have not heard from me since June. I have written regularly but suppose the letters have been lost.

I have been getting up a choir in our church here. We have a bass viol and two violins, and the singing is quite respectable. Mr. Mc-Carty is an excellent man and a devoted Christian. He behaved very well during the different actions, encouraging the men, telling them to "hurry up, keep their cartridges dry, and trust in God." The men had to cross ditches waist deep in water, which caused the remark about the cartridges.

I sent you several letters last week by the British Minister [Charles Bankhead], who has gone to Havana for his health. I enclosed you $300.00; write me if you get it, as if it is lost on the way, I can stop payments at the bank.

I do not know when I can come home, for General Scott will not let even the wounded go unless a surgeon gives a certificate that they cannot be able to do duty for at least three months. General Scott says that there are, of course, many applicants, some officers having been in the country for nearly two years; but he has so few officers that he cannot let the good ones go, and the bad ones shall not go. So under either head I see no chance.

As soon as [the Mexican] Congress meets we shall know what course it intends to pursue in regard to the war. There cannot be any more fighting of any consequence. I shall only have to be careful of my health, and that is excellent now. Of course I ran my chance with the rest during the late engagements. It is certainly a very exciting time during the raging of a battle; no one fears danger, and the greater it is, the greater the excitement. And very soon, even before the first engagement I entered into, I became so accustomed to seeing men fall, killed, or wounded around me that it did not even attract my attention. Strange, strange beings that we are! But the next day, in visiting the wounded at the hospitals, I could not bear the sight of the wounded, but would be obliged to go home. No one but an eyewitness can imagine the sight of a hospital after an action — trunks without limbs; a body with life not extinct, so mangled by shell that no one could recognize it, and the person himself incapable of telling his name. But it is all too horrible to refer to.

Some of the wounded officers are going to the United States by the train this letter goes on.

If I get a good opportunity I will send you the shawl which I bought for you on the 20th, the anniversary of our wedding day. I wonder how you spent that day.

I saw in the papers that a company of cavalry has been mustered into service at Alton [Illinois], on the 16th of last month. As there are few companies of mounted men on the road below, this [letter] will be retained at Puebla, probably.

I must ask a favor of you. It is to get me a small edition of the Prayer Book. When I came up, I left my trunk at Veracruz and most of my clothes. When I reached Perote, Mr. McCarty loaned me a Prayer Book, but it is so large and clumsy I would like to have a small one.

Major [Francis] Lee of the 4th Infantry and myself have made arrangements together. His wife, Mrs. Lee, lives at the St. Charles Hotel in New Orleans. She was a Miss Easton. Well, as letters are so irregular, whenever Mrs. Lee gets a letter from the major, she will drop you a line, as the major will, in his letters to her, mention me. So in case his letters go safe and mine do not, you can hear from me through her. And I promised to write to you to the same effect, so I shall hereafter speak of Major Lee in all my letters, and you must drop a line to Mrs. Lee and tell her. I think this is a good arrangement as so many letters are lost. Goodbye.

Your affectionate husband.

LETTER, October 31, 1847. Mexico City.

My Dearest Wife:

The train has been delayed some days by the road to Peñón having been rendered impassable by the Mexicans, who have dug ditches across it, and a few days ago some guerrillas drove off five hundred of our wagon mules. But the road has been mended and the train leaves in an hour, and a great many of our friends leave for the United States. The bidding goodbye to our companions who have fought with us in many battles, and particularly as they are going home, makes those who must remain here more desirous of going home ourselves. But our time will come soon, I hope.

I have nothing new to relate, but I am anxious to drop you a line at the last moment and tell you how kind God is to me in keeping me in such perfect health while so many are mere shadows and many of the officers are in bad health.

I sent you the shawl I bought for you. I sent it by [First] Lieutenant [Edward] Johnson of our regiment, who will leave it with Dr. McCormick at the St. Charles Hotel in New Orleans. So if you come down the river this winter you can get it.

The past four or five days have been quite cool. Nearly everybody is shivering and complaining, but I have enjoyed it, for I love the cold weather and always feel better than during the hot season. I hear occasionally an officer speak of bringing his family here.

We shall know soon whether our government intends holding out in the country. If this is the decision, I know, for one, that I am not going to spend my life here away from you, and I shall, accordingly, make arrangements to have you with me. Of course this will take time, but Congress will soon decide how to act.

How good you are to write so regularly, though I have not received all your letters. Remember me affectionately to all at home.

Ever your affectionate husband.

JOURNAL, November 1, 1847. Mexico City.

Today a large number of officers and a train have left the city for Veracruz, the officers to go thence to their homes. Most, if not all of them, are obliged to go on account of their health and wounds. It was sad to part with them, for our number is very small. And independent of their loss as companions in arms, who have been with us through many trying scenes, they go *home*, and are a connecting link between us and those whom we love. They will soon be happy in the embrace of their fathers, mothers, brothers, sisters, wives and children! Whilst we must still remain far away.

LETTER, November 6, 1847. Mexico City.

My Own Dear Kate:

How much I wish you were here to enjoy this delightful climate. I have the greatest desire for, and would be very pleased with more cold, but you would say it is charming. It is as mild and pleasant as June in the North. We will have plenty of fresh vegetables: peas, tomatoes, etc.; and fruits: bananas, oranges, pineapples, figs, etc. Flowers, too, are still in bloom, and the fields in the neighborhood of this city are green. It does not seem at all like autumn. It is the very place for you, and I often say to myself, "What a beautiful and happy country this might be if there were good laws and the people virtuous." But I suppose there is no nation on earth where there is so much wickedness and vice of all kinds. There is little incentive to virtue here. How little of that pure and holy religion which our blessed Savior taught is to be found in this country. No one could believe how low and depraved these people are, and instances are common of men selling their wives and sisters, and often their mothers and daughters. The clergy, generally, are very immoral and ready to stoop to the very lowest acts of villainy and wickedness.

I ride out of the city on horseback nearly every afternoon and often think how much you would be delighted with the magnificent views we have here of the snow-topped mountains. They rise out of a broad plain and tower above the clouds. The view at sunset is unequal to anything I ever saw. The snow during the day is of a dazzling whiteness, but at this hour it is a bright red, for the rays of the sun strike the mountains long after it has disappeared below the horizon.

I attended the opera a few nights ago and heard the favorite of Bellini's, "La Sonnambula." I feel very lonely at times but draw consolation from that religion which sustains us under all circumstances.

LETTER, November 7, 1847. Mexico City.

What are you doing today, I wonder? This is the first Sunday in the month, and Mr. McCarty administered the sacrament [of Communion] today. It is a solemn occasion at all times, but it seems to me it is more impressive since I came into Mexico, than ever. This evening is indeed lovely; the stars are all out, looking down so smiling, and the brightest of all is our star. I wonder if you watch it as much as I do. It is almost directly overhead now, and it is smiling upon both of us at the same time.

We parted in the springtime and now it is nearly winter. Think of the changes that have taken place at our own home at Fort Gibson. Indian summer has come and gone, and many delightful rides we took last year at this time. I think when we get settled in a home again, I shall not dare to trust you on horseback, for I often recall the ride on the 20th of this month last year when you came so near being killed. I had intended taking a Mexican pony home for you, but Colonel [Felix] Layton [of the Missouri Militia] took one home for his daughter, and she was thrown and killed. So I do not like the idea of trusting you on horseback again.

By the by, have you kept a journal? I began one and write in it occasionally and have now written nearly eighty pages.

I am getting out of patience with General Patterson, who was to bring us some mail, but he has hardly left Veracruz.[10] So we live in hope. I received your letter Number 24 some three weeks ago, while all between that number and Number 13 are behind.

We have a rumor today that commissioners are to meet Mr. Trist in four or five days and try again to see if peace cannot be made. I have but little hope of a favorable result, but I do hope and pray that peace will be brought about.[11]

LETTER, November 10, 1847. Mexico City.

No mail yet. I wish General Patterson was court-martialed. He has been expected here for the last month, and the last intelligence from him was that he had not left Veracruz. General Scott intends to send a column, immediately upon his arrival, to Querétaro [the temporary seat of the Mexican government], which is a city some one hundred and fifty miles northwest of this place. It is the capital of a state of the same name, and a congress has been in session there for some time for the purpose, so they say, of arranging matters for peace. But the rumor is that Santa Anna has made his appearance there and produced a revolution. I do not know who will be sent there, but a report says "Worth's Division." I would not object to this if it did not put more distance between us. If we do go, we will try hard to lay our hands on this rascal Santa Anna. He is too great a wretch to live. If the country could be rid of him we would soon have peace.

We are now getting our troops in good order again, drilling constantly. We had our brigade out yesterday in the plaza, but on account of the carriages and *léperos* [vagabonds] that throng the place, we are to go out about a mile where there is a fine drilling ground. I mounted my horse this afternoon to look for a place and succeeded in finding a fine, level plain reaching out a mile or two.

While I am writing this, Colonel Clarke is busily engaged talking with General Terrés. He is the Mexican general who commanded the Garita de Belén when we took the city. He is a Spaniard by birth and has been a soldier fifty years, he says. He was in the Peninsular War [1808–14] and is a brave officer. It is very amusing to hear them trying to understand each other, for Colonel Clarke, not being able to speak Spanish, is talking in bad French, and General Terrés does little better. [12]

I always love the autumn months, not the autumn in this country, for I like the frost to change the hues of the leaves, and I love to hear them drop, although not a breath of air moves. Oh, how lovely the northern autumn is! Some people pretend to believe an autumn spent in the country is horrible.

What would I not give to make a mount and drop down by your side at Alton. I know it is a beautiful place at this season of the year. Where is Aunt Julia? You know she said she would never return to Fort Gibson again. How willingly would I be ordered back there, and we would take our little cottage where we were so happy. And if we could get Aunt Hetty, and Joe, and the old brown cow, and the chickens, dogs, and the two cats, we would have our family together again. And I reckon all, from Aunt Hetty down to the cats, wish for their old master and mistress again. But referring to all this past happiness makes me discontented, and I will say goodnight. God bless you my beloved wife.

Affectionately, your husband.

JOURNAL, November 13, 1847. Mexico City.

A large party visited El Peñón today: Generals Scott, Twiggs, Pierce, Cadwalader, and Smith, with some one hundred or more officers. [13] We went out of the city by the *garita* de San Antonio and kept on that road until we came to Churubusco. After looking around some time at the place where the sanguine battle of the 20th August last was fought, we turned off to the left and passed through Mexicalzingo. From there [we went] on around Lake Texcoco and struck the main road from the east, on the other side of the Peñón, coming upon it as we would have done had we taken that road instead of turning off as we did on the 13th of August and going around Lake Chalco. Peñón is a large rock, rising, as it were, out of the lake. The road, which is a narrow causeway built up a few feet above the level of the lake, runs at the base of and to the right of the hill. This position is capable of a very strong defense, for there is but one way of approaching it, and from the embrasures there must have been at least twenty pieces of artillery bearing upon the road. There were several elevations rising one above the other, which would have rendered it almost impossible to have taken it with infantry—without great loss, as the sides of the mountain are so steep and rugged besides being covered by a dense growth of the cactus, that a storming party would stand a poor chance. After spending an hour or two examining this stronghold, we returned to the city, General Scott riding back in the Mexican state carriage.

JOURNAL, November 14, 1847. Mexico City.

Sunday. I went to church this morning; heard an excellent sermon by Mr. McCarty. In the afternoon we had to go to drill, the brigade being ordered out by General Worth. Whilst out it began to rain, and although we got a drenching, were satisfied as we were very much in want of rain, none having fallen during the last month. It is now the middle of November, still we have an abundance of green vegetables, potatoes, peas, beets, onions, cabbage, tomatoes, turnips, etc. Fruits also are plenty—apples, pears, oranges, bananas, pineapples, etc. Flowers are still in blossom, and the air is as mild and pleasant as early in September at the north. The mercury in a thermometer which hangs in our quarters remains nearly stationary at 60 or 65 [degrees] above zero.

LETTER, November 16, 1847. Mexico City.

My beloved wife:

I have one letter for you lying on my table, and if I should wait for a mail to go and only write then, you would get few letters. So I continue to write, as I promised. I have been thinking for some two or three days past that you received the letters which I sent by the

British Minister. He was in Veracruz the last of the month. I hope you have received them for I know your anxiety. General Scott sent an express off day before yesterday to Puebla with orders for a command to leave at once and bring up the mail, and we feel confident of getting it in the course of the present week. The British courier is expected in tonight from Veracruz; he may bring me a letter. I got one last month by him; this letter was written on the 8th of September, the day we were fighting at El Molino del Rey. Little did you think, when writing me then, that your husband was in the fiercest battle of this valley.

I wrote you in this last letter that our division would probably go to Querétaro; the report today is that General Smith will go with his division, but I presume General Scott has not decided who will go.

What has been done this fall about getting Gustavus [Gustave Mix] into the Military Academy? I hope he will succeed. I am going to see if I cannot do something. I have concluded to see General Pierce, and if he will only interest himself, [President James] Polk will give it to him, for General Pierce and Mr. Polk are good friends. General Pierce has been very kind to me, and it would afford me great pleasure to see Gustavus at West Point.

I wonder when we shall be able to visit New England. I am very anxious to introduce you to my parents and to my sisters and brother. My father will be fifty-six years old next January. My mother is about the same age, and I fear, lest we visit them soon, we shall never see mother for she cannot live long. We must go and visit them as soon as I get a furlough.

LETTER, November 18, 1847. Mexico City.

How happy I was tonight! We received the mail, and although I received no letters from home, that is New England, I received sixteen letters from my dear wife, and none missing. I have been busy all day reading them over and over. All the letters from Numbers 13 to 30, inclusive, have come safe to me.

I will bring you some Mexican shoes when I come, if I can find some that are pretty. The women here all have very small feet, but they pinch their feet still more which makes them look bad.

I have sent you $300.00. Have you received it? I wish I had a thousand to send. I also sent a box for you; Lieutenant Johnson took it and was to leave it with Dr. McCormick [in New Orleans]. I hope you have received it.

You need not worry about a servant [for me]. You are very kind, as well as [your] brother Alfred, in his willingness to send me one. I have Burroughs still, and he is a good hustler and does first rate to make my bed, etc. I have also an excellent laundress; she works and mends very nicely, and you will find when I make my appearance that I have managed to get along pretty well, considering, that is, as far as my clothes are concerned.

LETTER, November 19, 1847. Mexico City.

Dear Kate:

You see that I write a few lines every day. I hear this morning that another train will go down to Veracruz in about three weeks, and I must answer a great many letters. I received one from Colonel Loomis full of good advice, just such a letter as I like to get. The poor old Colonel would like to be here, I know, and he ought to be permitted to come. I received a letter from Flint, too. He says he has written me several times and wonders why I have never written him.[14]

I hope to be promoted in the course of a few months, not to a captaincy, but to a first lieutenant. This gives me $5.00 a month more pay. Magnificent, is it not?

I wonder whether you have decided to stay in Alton this winter, or stay in New Orleans. I hope you will do just as you feel inclined. From your letters you seem to be well situated and surrounded by those who love you. I must close now. I have but room to say God bless you. Your sincerely affectionate husband.

LETTER, November 26, 1847. Mexico City.

My Dearest Kate:

I am desirous of dropping a line to you at the last minute before the mail leaves. I have just been getting ready for the train and have written to Lieutenant Flint, Colonel Loomis, Dr. Hart, [your brother] Alfred, and I don't know how many others.[15]

I have little new to tell you. Don't feel any anxiety about me as nine-tenths of the stories you hear about us are not true. In your last letter you had us all killed off at Río Frío, etc., but I must tell you that I am in no more danger than if I were with you at Alton. Take good care of yourself, and I will do likewise. You wrote about my sleeping on the cold ground. No, indeed, I should get rheumatism and should be very cross in my old age. I have a fine mattress and a camp bedstead, and I have some fine, thick flannel shirts, and they are warm and nice. As for enjoying myself, I am famous for it.

I have a long row of flower beds with flowers in them too, and the old Spaniard [Colonel Deocamentes] who owns this house has entrusted them to my care. And his aviary with hundreds of canary birds in it I can enjoy as much as I please. There is a little wren who has her nest across the road under the eaves of the convent. She comes into my room and pecks crumbs off the floor.

I have drilling enough to do. This takes up the time and keeps me from ennui. I used to write a great deal, but now I have a couple of clerks and I keep them busy. I have lately gotten hold of a lot of books. They are novels, and they are good novels too. One is *The Cloth of Gold.* Have you ever read it? Another which I have just finished is one of Ellen Pickering's, *The Grumbler,* which interested me very much.[16]

I have made some acquaintances in this city. One of them is an Irish lady, a Mrs. O'Sullivan. She sent me yesterday a basket of apples and an apple pie.[17]

You ask why I do not send my letters to General Taylor's camp [in northern Mexico], that they would be more sure to go safely. We have had no communication with that part of the army except via New Orleans, so that cannot be. I hope, however, that you will be able to get letters from me more regularly, at least once a month, if not oftener.

General Pillow and Colonel Duncan are both in arrest [for insubordination].[18]

Have you received the shawl I sent you, and the money? Communication is so uncertain that I shall be anxious until I hear.

What do you think of coming to Mexico to live? There seems to be little prospect of the war ending, and everybody seems to think we are to retain possession of the whole country. While by so doing it may be right and for the best, but I doubt it. If you can join me here I shall be contented.

Begin a new series of letters at the first of January, at Number 1 again. There is no news here, and if it is necessary to make one [a letter] interesting, mine will not be so.

Remember me to all, and believe me, Your affectionate husband.

JOURNAL, November 28, 1847. Mexico City.

We are still waiting the arrival of General Patterson before General Scott sends off any troops to occupy the different states. A train went down, taking a mail, on the 1st of the month; it reached Veracruz on the 14th and is expected back in about a fortnight, when we will get a large mail. I sent a couple of letters to Kate by the British courier, who left this morning, and who goes through to Veracruz in 48 hours from this city.

I have been to church all day today. Miss Baygally, an English lady of my acquaintance, went with me this afternoon.

Colonel Clarke is now commanding the 1st Division, General Worth being in arrest.[19] This keeps me pretty busy. I go and turn off the division guards every morning at 8 o'clock. This I have no objection to, although it is growing quite cold in the mornings; the mercury has been down to 44 above zero for three mornings past.

JOURNAL, December 1, 1847. Mexico City.

Today is the first day of winter. I left New Orleans on the 11th of April; it was spring. The summer and the autumn are gone, and the winter is here. How fast the time has flown, and yet how many events have been crowded into those seven or eight months.

I have been out today with a small party and visited Tacuba. This is now a small town, but was once a large city. It is remarkable as having been the place to which Cortez and his army fled on the *noche triste* when they left this city. The bridge, or rather the canal, which Captain Alvarado, one of Cortez' greatest men, [leaped] is now within the limit of this city, and there is no canal or appearance of having been one, but the limits of the leap are still preserved in the road by the paving stones. Tacuba is about four miles to the west of the city, going out by the *garita* of San Cosme. There are a great many ancient ruins, showing the former size of the place.[20]

Cortez and his army on that eventful night passed on to the mountains, some twelve miles from the city; here on a high hill he fortified himself. And the discovery of the wax doll [the image of the Virgin] in the knapsack of one of his soldiers, which produced such wonderful effects upon the spirits of his men, gave a name to the place, or rather to the convent which he built on his return from Tlaxcala: Nuestra

Señora de los Remedios. This image is second [in number of devo-
tees] only to the Virgin of Guadalupe.[21]

We left Tacuba and went off to the left, coming in by Chapultepec.
On our way we found a hacienda with a flour mill attached; it was
a beautiful place. The owner came out and invited us to go into his
house and offered us refreshments, but we declined as it was getting
to be late. We saw here a llama which he told us he obtained from
South America; it was very tame and his children rode it about the
place. I here had my eyes gratified by a small grove of cottonwood
trees which this gentleman told us he brought from the United States.

JOURNAL, December 4, 1847. Mexico City.

A large party went out today and visited Contreras. Generals Twiggs
and Smith, Colonel Riley, and some fifty other officers composed the
party. Contreras lies some fifteen miles about south in direction from
this city. We went to San Angel and from there to the village of Contreras, in the neighborhood of which lies the battleground.

On the 19th of August, General Valencia was entrenched on the
slope of a hill running towards San Agustín. In Valencia's rear, across
a deep ravine at a distance of some two miles, lay General Santa Anna
with a large army. The Mexican force outnumbered our entire army
some three to one, and not more than five thousand [Americans] were
in this vicinity on the morning of the 20th. Riley's brigade passed up
the ravine which ran between Valencia and Santa Anna and reached
the summit in rear of the works which Valencia had thrown up.[22]

At daybreak the charge was made. As soon as they were discovered, the guns were turned, but owing to the downward slope, they
fired over the heads of our troops, and in seventeen minutes by the
watch (so General Smith told me), the enemy was completely routed.
As soon as the large body [of Mexican troops], which ought to have
come down and cut off Riley's command, saw Valencia routed, off
it went joining in the retreat, blocking the road, and were shot down
in hundreds. On the slope alone five hundred were killed. It was a
glorious day for our little army, for the night before there was a gloom
and a sadness upon our officers and men, seeing so large a body of
the enemy and so well fortified. It was dark and rainy besides very
cold. It is called the "*triste noche*" [sad night] of our campaign.

We returned home by way of San Agustín, San Antonio, and Churubusco. These places all looked familiar to me, recalling to memory the sanguinary scenes of the 20th August last.

JOURNAL, December 5, 1847. Mexico City.

Sunday. I have been to church twice today. It is the first Sunday of the month, and Mr. McCarty administered the holy communion. There were some twenty-five partakers, most of them officers, although there were a few citizens.

LETTER, December 5, 1847. Mexico City.

My Dear Kate:

The train has been delayed some days, but I believe it is to start tomorrow, so I must not let this opportunity pass. I sent two letters by the British courier which left more than a week ago. I wish you would tell me in your letters the number of my letters that you receive. I suspect that all those I have sent by private couriers have been lost.

We are all anxiously waiting to see what policy our government is going to pursue and what effect it will have on the Mexicans. They certainly know by this time that we are in earnest, for we hear by the arrival of an express from Veracruz that four thousand more men are to be sent into the country besides those now here. So in a short time, I think, we shall know whether we shall remain here a few months or for the next fifteen years. Now if you were here, I should not care how long the war lasted, and as soon as we are at all settled you had better make up your mind to join me. I will give you plenty of time to prepare for the journey and perhaps will come and get you; but you must wait patiently and see what will turn up.

Colonel Clarke has command of General Worth's division since his arrest. This keeps me a little more busy, but I never complain of having too much employment. I never have so much to do that I do not find plenty of leisure — I require to be kept busy.

I have a plan which I have been thinking over for some time and if we could only carry it out I should be delighted. I do not know but that you will laugh at me when I tell you what it is. I wish I had the means to carry it into operation. It is to save a little from our pay each year, enough in amount in a few years to buy a farm, and then at some future day, when we feel inclined, we could leave the army and have a home. There are many officers who are now broken down in health, and had they taken this precaution, they would now have a place of their own to retire to. You know if we once begin to lay up something, no matter how small a sum the first year, it will be easier the next, and after a few years we would have sufficient to buy this little farm. Well, shall we begin next month, that is, the beginning of the year? I have been trying to be very economical and will continue to do so and see if we cannot save something.

I am in hopes of getting promoted this winter in some way. If I could only get to be captain I should be glad, and I do not think it altogether unlikely that I may not be so promoted. In the first place the position I have occupied since I have been in the field, that of assistant adjutant-general, may be the means of my getting an appointment, which would of course increase our little means. Then we could lay up something, and how pleased I would be if we had a place of our own; we will have it some of these days if kind Providence smiles on us — not a palace, but it will be a home. I am very willing to be busy for I am not naturally idle; I do not care how much I have to do, but let me have my own fireside and my wife, and I will be contented. In your next letter you must give me your views on this subject for I will not take a step unless you agree with me. So tell me your thoughts on the subject, and perhaps you can suggest something I have not thought of.

I am perfectly delighted with the climate here. For the last week it has been real winter weather, and some persons say they have seen ice, but I have not. Still it is just cold enough to be comfortable. The colonel complains all the time, but I have got my thick dragoon overcoat, which is double lined, and this I wear when I go out guard-mounting every morning, and at night I sleep under four blankets.

I have almost finished my letter and I have given you no news, but there is none here; we all live quietly. There is occasionally an officer tried, or a duel, or some other event of that kind, but no movements of troops and there will not be probably until about New Year's. General Patterson has not arrived, and it is hard to tell when we will expect him. Well, goodbye. Remember me to Dr. Hart and sister Sophie.

Ever your affectionate husband.

P.S. The train has not gone, but leaves today. General Patterson has at last arrived at Puebla, and General Lane is expected here in a day or two with a large body of troops and a big mail, and I wonder how many letters I shall get. [23]

I have not heard from home [Springfield, Massachusetts] since last July. Your last letter was written on the 13th of October, quite recent compared with the letters which some of the officers have received from their families; some of them have not heard from their wives since last summer. I thought of you yesterday when I went to church, for I always take you to church with me because I carry your miniature in my pocket. You have become quite a traveler, having been in all the battles of the Valley [of Mexico] except Contreras.

When General Lane arrives with the train, General Scott is going to reorganize the troops, and the question now is who is going to stay here in the City of Mexico. I suppose by far the greater number will be scattered over the whole country. A week or two will decide, and my next letter may be from Oaxaca or some other place.

I presume you will receive this letter by New Year's, and I wish you a very happy one. When this anniversary rolls around again, may we be together!

How many years will it take to purchase our farm, and where shall we locate it? A good long way off from any city, for I do love the country, the bright green fields with everything around you that is lovely and beautiful. Living in the city is almost like living in prison to me. Now, do not forget to write what you think about the farm, for I really am in downright earnest, never so much before in all my life. I believe I will write [Lieutenant] Flint and persuade him to have a farm adjoining ours. That will be capital, will it not?

JOURNAL, December 7, 1847. Mexico City.

We received a mail today by the arrival of General Patterson, who came into the city with Colonel [John C.] Hays and 500 mounted Texans. The newspaper mail was very large as we had received no papers before [*sic*] since last August.

JOURNAL, December 8, 1847. Mexico City.

General Cushing with some 1,500 troops arrived today; among them were [men of] the Massachusetts Regiment of [U.S.] Volunteers. [24]

JOURNAL, December 9, 1847. Mexico City.

A train left today for Veracruz. The 1st Artillery went down as escort. This regiment is to remain there and the 1st Infantry to return. Many officers and men went out by this train; most of them were wounded in the late actions. The report about town today is that the troops are to be reorganized, and as soon as General Butler arrives, two columns of 4,000 men each are to be sent off, one to Querétaro and the other to San Luis [Potosí].[25]

LETTER, December 9, 1847. Mexico City.

Katie Dear:

I am sure you will get tired of my letters for they do not contain any news, but since I last wrote I have received four letters from you.

General Patterson has at last made his appearance with five hundred men. This is the first addition we have had.

I have received your letters numbered 23, 31, 32, and 33. You know that 23 has been missing a long time, but now I have all your letters from 31 to 33. Am I not lucky? But you write as late as October 22 that you do not hear from me. How can this be, for I have written [at] every opportunity, and it grieves me to think you have not had a word from me for so long. But I am sure you must have heard by this time, for the letters I sent by the English Minister reached Veracruz before the last of October. There is a strange fatality in these mails, for while all your letters have arrived safely, I have not heard one word from my father or anyone in Springfield for nearly six months, and I know they have written regularly.

I received today a number of the *Hampton Post* and the *Christian Witness*. Do not stop sending them for I receive them all.

How much I wish you could be here. I love a soldier's life because I am a soldier, and as long as I remain in the army I am proud of my profession. But had I some other which would give us a home and sufficient to "make the pot boil," to use a homely phrase, I should be far happier, and a farm is the only thing I can think of which would give us the wished-for change.

You say in your last letters that you are coming to join me, that I shall be surprised to see you make your appearance. Do not venture to take the step until you hear from me, for as soon as it is practical I shall come or send for you. But remember, there is not a lady in the field, and the destination of the different regiments is a matter of uncertainty. It would make some difference even if there were some accommodations on the road from here to Veracruz, but you would have to travel with the troops, making twelve or fifteen miles a day, stopping at night with no shelter but a tent, and you would suffer more than you have any idea of. If we occupy this country, you shall come out as soon as you can do so in safety, and I trust kind Providence will again permit us to meet. How kind He has been to us in all our separation, and we will continue to trust in Him and all will yet be well.

I know you must have passed many hours of suspense and anxiety in not hearing from me, but I hope it is all over now, and I feel confident there will be no more fighting. The Mexican army is entirely disorganized and the country has no means for raising another. So any uneasiness about me is entirely unnecessary. If you see any rumors in the papers take them for what they are. A few days will decide whether I am to go into the interior or to the country.

I will not write more now. I hope you are going to St. Louis soon. God bless you.

Ever your affectionate husband.

LETTER, December 16, 1847. Mexico City.

My Dearest Kate:

The British courier has come in and I was not fortunate enough to get any letters. But as our train, which left Veracruz just after General Butler [did], is expected in a few days, I must be patient.

Well, how about our farm? Do you think you would like to own one? I am forming many plans to be carried into execution when we are independent. One of the greatest pleasures that I will have will be to have my father and mother visit us. I cannot calculate how long it will be before we will realize enough to have a farm, but I think it will not take more than ten years. We are still young. I am twenty-six, and if we shall decide ten years hence to take this step, we will be young enough to begin farming. This idea has taken such a hold upon me that I have been reading for the last week all the papers about sowing grain, raising sheep, etc., and I am sure I could make a capital farmer. What life is more happy and independent than that of a farmer? I have been talking so much about our farm that I have not told you any news.

There has been a reorganization and we are all broken up. Our division, which was composed of the 2nd and 3rd Regiments of Artillery, and 5th, 6th, and 8th Infantry, of regulars and veteran troops, has been broken up. We are now under General Cadwalader, and our division is composed of the 4th Artillery, and the 1st, 6th, 8th, 9th, and 11th Regiments of Infantry. The two latter regiments are [U.S.] Volunteers. Colonel Clarke goes out by the first train which leaves in a few days, and I go to my regiment, no longer doing the duties of assistant adjutant-general, but go to my old duties as adjutant of the 6th.

I feel quite sad about the breaking up of our mess. Colonel Clarke, Mr. McCarty, Lieutenant Burwell, and myself commenced messing together nearly eight months ago. Poor Burwell was killed, and Colonel Clarke goes home. Mr. McCarty will probably remain in this city, and I will probably start for Zacatecas in two or three weeks. Colonel Clarke's health is not good, and General Scott told him tonight either to go home or to Jalapa as governor of the department. Had he gone there, I should have gone too and could have sent directly for you, but the colonel thought his health required a visit home, and he is going.

It is hard to break up as the colonel has been very kind to me. He told me that he should visit Washington and that he would do all he could to get me brevetted. He says I deserve two brevets, and he will use all his influence to get both. I would like this, for it would make me a captain. He also complimented me very highly and said he would recommend me to the adjutant-general for the appointment of assistant adjutant-general. If he was made brigadier general (and I presume he will be), he will be entitled to an aide-de-camp, and he told me that he would write to me in this case and offer it to me. If all this happens, and he gets a command in the United States, I will accept; but to use a homely phrase, "We must not count our chickens, etc." As this was very kind of Colonel Clarke, you must not speak about it, for perhaps I shall not get anything.

I met an old friend today, Lieutenant [Daniel O.] Regan, who belongs in the [1st] Massachusetts Regiment [of Volunteers], and he used to live in Springfield. He left there last February, not a year ago, and saw my father and has told me a thousand things about the changes among my friends. I was very glad to see him, and more so because he saw my father so lately.

Tomorrow I move out of my quarters and to my regiment. Captain Hoffman will command [the Sixth]. I shall either mess with him or with Captain Cady, who by the way is not dead as was reported; he is as lively and clever as ever.

About our future movements we are uncertain. Two columns of about three thousand men each are to go as far as Querétaro, where they separate, one for San Luis Potosí and the other for Zacatecas, where we shall probably go. But it will make no difference to me. You must direct letters in the future to "Adjutant, 6th Infantry, General Cadwalader's Division." The letters are all put up in packages at Vera-cruz for each regiment, and if you neglect to put on the number of the regiment, the letters will not reach me. I feel quite homesick since the new arrangement, for I was so well satisfied before. But I suppose it is all for the best, and I must make the most out of it. Goodnight. I will write again before the mail leaves.

Your ever affectionate husband.

JOURNAL, December 17, 1847. Mexico City.

I moved down from my quarters opposite San Francisco [church] to-day and reported to Captain Hoffman. Our division, as well as the others, has been broken up, and a new reorganization made. Captain Hoffman has kindly invited me to mess with him, and I have accepted the offer. I have a room in the convent of San Fernando. The quarters are cold and cheerless; I prefer by far my old ones, but a soldier can-not often consult his own wishes and convenience.[26]

JOURNAL, December 18, 1847. Mexico City.

General Butler arrived today with some three or four thousand men. But he brought no mail; it will be here in two or three days by Colonel Johnson, who is believed with the train which left [Veracruz] on the 1st of November.[27]

LETTER, December 18, 1847. Mexico City.

Well, here I am quartered in Number 21, Convent of San Fernando. I have broken up mess with the colonel [Clarke] and am now with my regiment and mess with Captain Hoffman. My room is very comfortable for a soldier or a monk; but I see the name of "Santa María Magdalena" on the door, which makes me think it has been the home of some nun, but she must have been rather cold here for there is no [glass] window, and I have to shut the blinds to keep warm. But my duties call me out most of the day, and it matters little at night. I have a furnace and a little charcoal brought in; this warms the room.

Colonel Clarke told me he would try to have Colonel Loomis brought out here to take command of my regiment. I only wish he was here; I should feel a little more contented than I now do. I shall try to get out of the country in the spring. I am sure I am entitled to a furlough even now, but there are so many officers who have been here since the breaking out of the war that my claims will not be admitted. I am anxiously looking forward to the time when I can get back. You will not find me changed, that is in character, except that I have grown a little wiser and love the finer side of life more than ever.

Tomorrow we get a mail. General Butler arrived today. His troops, numbering some six or eight thousand, began coming into the city yesterday, and tomorrow Colonel Johnson, of the [Louisiana] Volunteers, who left on the first of November, will be here.

I have not told you that it is General Scott's opinion that we will have peace in three months. I do not know upon what grounds he bases this opinion, but let us hope it may be well founded. Only think of the many glad hearts that peace would make!

There is one thing that I enjoy in my new quarters which I was deprived of before — I can look out of the window at the end of a long gallery and see our star.

Goodbye again. I will write in a few days.

JOURNAL, December 19, 1847. Mexico City.

Attended church twice today. Mr. McCarty gave us two excellent sermons. The text in the morning was "Thou art the man," and a plain, practical sermon it was. I sincerely hope and pray that we may not lose our chaplain if we go to Zacatecas. I am afraid we shall have none, for Mr. McCarty thinks he shall remain here, as he can probably do more good, as a greater number of troops will be in this city than in any other place, besides the great number of sick in the hospitals.

JOURNAL, December 25, 1847. Mexico City.

Christmas. Mr. McCarty gave us a sermon this morning, and although far away from those I love, still I had the kind privilege of partaking of the Lord's supper. I sincerely hope my beloved Kate was also permitted to receive this blessing.

After service I went with some other officers and called on Generals Scott, Worth, Smith, Cadwalader, Butler, and others. And finally I ended the day by dining with the ordnance officers Captains Huger, Hagner, Lieutenants Laidley and Stone, and Dr. Randall. We had a fine dinner, fresh salmon, oysters, etc. General Scott told us he believed we should be on our way home by April next. I really hope and pray he is correct in his opinion.[28]

I visited the house of a Spanish gentleman last evening. He had quite a party of officers, some gentlemen besides the officers, and fifteen or twenty ladies. It was a celebration of the birth of our Saviour. A room was fitted up in tasteful style, representing the stable in which were Mary and Joseph. [An image of] the little child was taken with great ceremony and laid in the manger. After this performance, there was dancing; one young lady sang a few airs, and with much sweetness of voice. The evening ended with a supper. All were agreeably entertained.

Christmas has been kept here pretty much as we keep it at home, plenty of eggnog and apple toddy, and any quantity of drunken [U.S.] Volunteers in the streets. Where might I spend next Christmas? A year ago I was on this day at my own home with my darling wife with me, and I trust next year I shall again have her with me.

LETTER, December 25, 1847. Mexico City.

My Dearest Kate:

A merry Christmas to you and I know you wish one to me, but it is hard enough for me to feel contented without being at all merry.

The train which went on to Veracruz on the 1st of November has returned, and though I was very much disappointed getting no letters, I was glad to get my trunk which I had left there. In looking it over I was reminded of you a thousand times. I found my dressing gown, my flute, my music box, my prayer book, and many other things which I was glad to get. Although the train was two weeks at Vera-cruz, there was not an arrival of a vessel from New Orleans during the whole time. I hope to hear that you have received my letters which I sent by the English Minister in October. I think it must have reached you about the 20th of November.

I have now been with my regiment, doing duty, for a week and get along very well. I could be very well contented in Mexico if you were only here. I am anxious to hear from you since winter set in. You are such a southern bird that you will shut yourself up in the house.

LETTER, December 27, 1847. Mexico City.

I have heard some good news. I called on General Scott to pay my respects, and he said we will all go home in April. He spoke very confidently of a speedy peace. The new party which has just come into power [in Mexico] has decided in favor of peace, and I judge, from what I hear, that an express has gone to Washington with terms from the Mexican government. It is willing to accept the ultimatum which Mr. Trist offered. This is very encouraging, is it not? We have received the President's message. This will influence the Mexicans some, undoubtedly.

I must describe the party I attended on Christmas Eve. Mr. Pizarro, a Spanish gentleman, invited our regiment to go to his house.[29] The officers, most of them, went. We found the house full of ladies and gentlemen. The ladies were well-dressed, some of them magnificently, and one or two were quite pretty. The evening's ceremony commenced by forming a procession. Each carried a wax candle, the leading couple carrying a little wax image of the Saviour Christ. After marching through the gardens, which were lighted by different colored lamps suspended in the orange trees, we marched into the house, through a room which had been dressed to represent the stable, and the child was deposited in the manger, the company singing hymns all the time. After this there was dancing, and the party broke up about 3 o'clock in the morning, after an elegant supper had been served. I retired and was sound asleep by 12 o'clock, myself. You know I do not dance and I soon got tired.

Christmas was kept very much as it is in our country, that is among the army. I called upon Generals Scott, Worth, Cadwalader, Butler, and Smith. We found plenty of egg and toddy, eggnog, etc. I dined with the ordnance officer, Captain Huger, and a classmate of mine, Lieutenant Laidley. We had fresh oysters and salmon, besides a dozen other dishes.

I do not know when I shall hear from you. We hear nothing from the troops below [between Mexico City and Veracruz].

I almost forgot to tell you that I do not believe I shall go out of this city, for one regiment, the 9th, of our brigade, has been ordered to the mines, and it will be gone until the last of January.[30] If we are to go, it will not be probably until the first of March. Before that time I am hoping peace will send us in another direction.

Only think of not hearing one word from my father for six months; I know he has written, but no letters have reached me. The last I heard was from you just after he had written you to inquire about me. I write regularly home, every opportunity. This letter will go by courier, who leaves here in the morning, and I hope you will receive it in the course of three weeks. I have written to Colonel Loomis within a few days. Goodbye.

May God bless you is the constant prayer of your affectionate husband.

JOURNAL, January 5, 1848. Mexico City.

Tomorrow morning at 8 o'clock we leave this city for the west. Our brigade, composed of the 4th Artillery, 6th, 8th, and 11th Infantry, goes to garrison Toluca, a city some sixteen or eighteen leagues [forty-five miles] southwest of this city. We are anticipating no resistance, but we may have more fighting; the Mexicans say we shall, but I sincerely hope and pray it is all over. If we do go again into battle, may God give us strength to do our duty as Christians and soldiers.

CHAPTER FIVE

Toluca, Popocatepetl, and Home

♣

JOURNAL, January 6, 1848. Jesús del Monte.

We left Mexico [City] this morning at 8 o'clock, having formed in the plaza. Captain [Edward J.] Steptoe's battery [the third Artillery] and two companies of the 1st Dragoons, Captain [Philip R.] Tompkins's and Lieutenant [Richard S.] Ewell's having been assigned to our brigade. We marched past General Scott's quarters; he stood on the balcony as we passed and received our salute. We are encamped to-night at Jesús del Monte, about twelve or fourteen miles from Mexico [City].

JOURNAL, January 8, 1848. Toluca.

We arrived in Toluca, the capital of the state of Mexico, this morning, having marched from Lerma, some ten miles, where we encamped last night.[1] A regiment is to return and occupy Lerma. Toluca is a very pretty little place containing some twenty-four thousand inhabitants in the city and adjoining villages. There was no opposition on the road, and the citizens seem disposed to treat us very kindly. The men are very comfortably quartered, and the officers have been billeted out among the inhabitants.

Captain Hoffman and myself are living at the house of a gentleman who treats us very hospitably and kindly. He has given us seats at his table, and we are living in the true Spanish style, chocolate in the morning as we rise. This is to last us until 12 o'clock when breakfast is served. With soup, this meal is a very substantial one, having some eight or ten courses of meats and vegetables. The dessert is fruit and sweetmeats. At five o'clock, chocolate or coffee with bread is again brought in. At seven or a little past, dinner is announced; this meal, like the breakfast, is also substantial, and is the meal of the day. I observed, among other dishes, one made of the pumpkin or squash, preserved; it made a very rich sweetmeat, although the taste of the pumpkin was not altogether gone. Its appearance was very much like preserved ginger. In eating their soup, I observed the Mexicans ate bananas, sliced. In all the dishes, meats and vegetables, a great abundance of chili or pepper is used, and little or no salt. One dish was certainly a novelty, being composed entirely of vegetables, more particularly green peas, and was made in the shape of and baked like a pie.

There is plenty of fruit and vegetables of all kinds to be had here. The valley of Toluca is one of the best in the world, being far superior to that of Mexico in richness and extent. The whole country from Lerma to this place is all under cultivation. The soil is very rich, and with little or no manning produces fine crops of corn, barley, wheat, etc.

JOURNAL, January 20, 1848. Toluca.

We have been here now upwards of two weeks. We are very pleasantly located, receive the city papers from Mexico early, by the diligence. Today we were very much gratified by the arrival of a mail under a small escort of dragoons from Mexico. I was fortunate enough to get letters from home, from my wife, and from Colonel Loomis. The latest date from my beloved wife was December 23, only one month ago! I cannot express my gratitude to my Heavenly Father for all His mercies to me in protecting me and restoring my dearest Kate to health, weighing 99½ lbs., [that is] more than she has weighed for many years. At my New England home all are well, and my sister Jeanette writes from Virginia that she is also enjoying herself.[2] May my Heavenly Father permit me to return soon and visit all my dear friends and relatives.

JOURNAL, February 10, 1848. Toluca.

We are now living in the hope of soon seeing peace established between Mexico and the United States. Commissioners on the part of Mexico have met Mr. Trist [the American commissioner], and some terms have been agreed upon and sent to the United States for ratification. We think it possible that some of us might leave the country this spring, but I am afraid to hope, but I am quite sure of going home in the fall, and that will be only eight or nine months at farthest.

99

JOURNAL, February 12, 1848. Toluca.

A party of us visited today the highest peak of the mountain which overhangs this city. Captains Hoffman and Alexander, Lieutenants Hancock, Buckner, Armistead, and myself composed the party. The height is about 2,000 feet above the city, and the view is very extensive and it is really magnificent. We propose forming a party and going up to the snow mountain which lies some fifteen or twenty miles off.[3]

JOURNAL, March 1, 1848. Toluca.

We received the mail from Mexico yesterday, and all were made glad by letters from those whom we love. I received one from my dear wife [written] as late as January 14th.

I had a conversation this evening with Dr. Franco, a Spanish gentleman who is a very intelligent and interesting gentleman. He gave me long accounts of General Alvarez, who is a mulatto, his mother being a negress from the Pacific Coast, and his father a Spaniard. He is personally very brave but is nothing of a general. He has a hacienda and a large estate on the borders of the *tierra caliente* [hot land], which is so extensive that it embraces no less than the torrid, temperate, and frigid zones. From Dr. Franco's account, I think it must be a most delightful location.[4]

JOURNAL, March 3, 1848. Toluca.

We received orders last night to go to Mexico [City] as soon as we are relieved by the Voltigeurs and the 14th Infantry. General Butler has reorganized the troops, giving General Worth his old division, composed of the 2nd and 3rd Artillery, the 4th, 5th, 6th, and 8th Regiments of Infantry, and Duncan's battery.[5] We would prefer, most of us, to remain here as it is very healthy and in the country. It is now very sickly in the city of Mexico, and although I do not dread it myself, still I, by far, prefer being here where the air is pure, and in three minutes one can be in the midst of broad, green fields and out of the reach of the sickness and vice of the town. But we must go to Mexico, and perhaps from there home. General Scott says it is his opinion that we shall be on our way by the first of May. God grant that it may prove so.

JOURNAL, March 5, 1848. Toluca.

Today is the first Sunday in the month, but as we have no chaplain, I have not been permitted to go to the house of God and partake of the divine sacrament of the Lord's Supper. But on the next return of this day, I hope to enjoy this privilege.

The day has been a grand fête day here. It is now Carnival, and besides the usual religious ceremonies, there were processions and bands of music in the streets, accompanied by persons masked, and in the afternoon there was a bullfight, which was attended by *tout le monde.* Some of the officers went and described the scenes as being really brutal, as no less than four bulls were cruelly killed, and two horses were so much gored that they probably died.

The prospects for peace seem to be very encouraging at present. All seem to believe that we shall be on our way to the United States by the 1st of May. This is very cheering to one who, after a sweet companionship of five months with a lovely girl, has been separated now almost a year. This gentle being, who was to me a guardian angel when together, has also been one to me when far away, for her influence, so mild, so gentle, and so lovely, has ever been present with me. I have used all my Christian patience and philosophy to be content with this dispensation of my Heavenly Father, and I have derived from the following extract, which recently met much satisfaction, the idea always believed, but I now meet it so beautifully expressed.

"Could the veil which now separates us from futurity be drawn aside, and those regions of everlasting happiness and sorrow which strike so faintly on the imagination be presented fully to our eyes, it would occasion, I doubt not, a sudden and strange revolution in our estimate of things. Many are the distresses, for which we now weep in suffering or sympathy, that would awaken us to songs of thanksgiving, many the dispensations, which now seem dreary and inexplicable, that would fill our adoring hearts with thanksgiving and joy." John Bowdler.[6]

Undoubtedly this is true, but until this veil is drawn aside, we must continue to weep in suffering and sympathy. But amid all the cares, the toils, the sufferings and temptations which surround us here, may I so live, pure in thought, feeling, word and deed, that I shall finally reach Heaven where, with my angel wife, I shall wander along "those rivers of pleasure which flow o'er the bright plains," and where, I doubt not, we shall enjoy all the beautiful things of earth. Even our flowers will be there, and like everything else seen through angel eyes, will be presented to us in a perfected form, and a thousand times far happier and glorious state of existence.

JOURNAL, March 12, 1848. Tacubaya.

Our regiment left Toluca on the morning of the 10th and, dividing the distance, arrived here yesterday. General Worth is here and commands the division, which is the only one quartered here. We were in Toluca two months and lost but three men, and they undoubtedly would have died anywhere else. We left no man behind us. We were relieved by the Voltigeurs and the 12th Infantry. The 8th [Infantry] will probably be in today, as they were to leave the day after us.

JOURNAL, March 23, 1848. Tacubaya.

We have this evening heard that the English courier had arrived from Veracruz, and that the treaty had been ratified. With the exception of one article, relating to Texas land claims, it has been accepted as it was sent from the commissioners. So we are all anxious to see what the Mexican Congress will do, and a few days now will decide whether or not we are to go home this spring.[7]

The Court of Inquiry in General Pillow's case has been very interesting for a few days past. The evidence is very amusing, and the case produces much interest.

We have had division drills all the week, preparatory to a grand review by General Butler, which is to come off on the 26th, Sunday morning, at 9 o'clock.

We had a mail three days ago from the United States. I received letters from my dear wife as late as the 24th ultimo, and from my father about the same date. Arrangements have been made to give us a mail twice a month, also for sending a mail to Veracruz twice monthly.

JOURNAL, March 26, 1848. Tacubaya.

General Butler reviewed our division today. Generals Cushing, Smith, and I [as adjutant general] do not know how many men were present, and the troops were in splendid order. After General Worth had drilled a little while to show off his division, he invited all the officers to his house, where he had a collation spread, and as there was plenty of wine, etc., the party was soon in a very merry mood. And all went home perfectly satisfied with General Worth's division, as well as with themselves.

JOURNAL, April 1, 1848. Tacubaya.

We received letters today by the arrival of a small mail. I heard from my beloved wife and from home, and all are well.

JOURNAL, April 3, 1848. Tacubaya.

Yesterday we received [official] news of the [American] ratification of the treaty, and it is believed here that Mexico will also accept it.

A party has been formed for visiting Popocatepetl. We have made all our arrangements and start this morning. I suppose we will number, officers and men, about seventy or eighty. We have an indefinite leave and shall probably be gone ten or twelve days. We are anticipating much pleasure from the excursion.

JOURNAL, April 15, 1848. Tacubaya.

Our party rendezvoused at the Citadel in Mexico [City] on Monday the 3rd for the purpose of starting on our expedition to Popocatepetl. We had engaged mules from a Mexican, as the roads would be frequently narrow and unfrequented, and we would find difficulty in getting along with wagons. But we were disappointed, as is always the case when you deal with Mexicans. So we packed our provisions, bedding, etc., in two public wagons furnished by the quartermaster. Our party numbers some twenty officers from the different corps of the Army, a few citizens, and an escort of about seventy dragoons and footmen. We had an indefinite leave of absence in order that we might accomplish our object. The first night a portion of our party stopped at Ayotla and the remainder at a hacienda in the neighborhood, some two or three miles off.

The second day we reached Tlalmanalco, a town of some five or six thousand inhabitants. Our direction was southeasterly as our object was to reach the neighborhood of the mountain at its southern slope, as the only practical route was there, in ascending.

On leaving Tlalmanalco, we passed through Miraflores ("See the flowers"), a village where there is a large cotton factory superintended by Mr. [J. H.] Robertson [of the Miraflores Textile Company], a Scotchman who entertained us very hospitably. The machinery in this establishment was made in Paterson, New Jersey. We reached the town of Amecameca that night. We concluded to leave our wagons here as the road for them farther on was impracticable. So we called on the *alcalde* [mayor], who furnished us with pack mules. He told us, when we applied for them, he would have them ready in two hours. At the expiration of that time the messenger returned and said the owner would not let the mules go, as we had not agreed upon the price to be paid. This was soon agreed upon, and after two hours more, they brought in the mules. And we traveled on that afternoon to Ozumba, where we were comfortably quartered by the *alcalde*.

On the fourth day we started quite early, reaching the small town of Atlautla, some two miles in the direction of the mountains, by eight o'clock. We obtained two guides here; they were stout young men who said they knew the way, as they had been up the mountain before with other parties which had visited the summit. Soon after leaving this village, our road was gradually ascending, all day. The path was made by the mules upon which the Indians bring wood down into the valley. Sometimes it was very steep, and we were delayed by the mules which occasionally met with some accident, getting their loads off, or rolling down the precipices. However, at 3 o'clock we reached the *vacaría* [cattle yard], which is a small clearing with a house or two where the Indians stay when they come up from the plains to graze their cattle in the neighborhood.

We were now about four thousand feet above the valley, and it was quite cold, but we were soon comfortable around large pine fires. The view from our camp was very extensive, and towards sunset it was very magnificent and grand, for above us on the mountain there was a severe snowstorm. Where we were, and in the whole plain to the south, the sun was shining brightly, whilst to our right towards Mexico [City], and far below us, the country was enveloped in a heavy thunder shower. Before 8 o'clock the storm from above had reached us, and we had sleet and snow during the whole night. We decided before retiring to attempt the ascent next morning.

The ground was covered with snow and the weather quite unsettled; however, we started soon after daylight. We reached the limit of vegetation after a distance of about three miles. We were now, we judged, some five thousand feet below the summit, and the ascent became more difficult as we advanced. Soon the wind increased and we were enveloped in the snow clouds. It was very cold, and we could not see a stone's throw in advance. We pushed on, determined to overcome all obstacles. By one o'clock our party, which numbered when starting from camp about thirty, had become reduced to five. The remainder had turned back one by one as they became exhausted by cold and fatigue. One of the officers came so near freezing that he would go neither one way nor the other, but lay down in the snow to sleep. As we had succeeded this far in ascending not more than one-third of the height, and the day being more than half gone, we concluded to return to camp and make a second trial on a fair day. We reached camp about 4 o'clock, having been upwards of five hours in a freezing snowstorm.

We soon found that the fatigues of climbing were but a small part of our difficulties, for one officer had his nose frozen, and several found their fingers frostbitten. This discouraged us somewhat, still we made arrangements to make another effort the next morning. Soon one began to complain of a pain in the eyes, and before dark every one of the party who had been exposed was suffering from a severe inflammation of the eyes. Our camp presented a singular scene that night and next morning. The pain was so intense that the sufferers could not sleep, consequently the whole camp was awake, the well ones trying every expedient our limited means afforded to alleviate the pain.

In the morning, as there were some twenty of our party who could not see, it was decided to descend into the valley and there await their recovery. As we went down the mountain our appearance was truly laughable, some fifteen of us so blind that, with bandages around their heads to keep the light from their eyes, they were led down. The descent being sometimes very abrupt and the trail windy, they groped their way like blind persons. We left two Italians in camp who had come out with us from Mexico, but who had not made the attempt with us on the preceding day. They were yet to make the trial, and as the day was fair, they thought they would succeed. We encamped that night at the base of the mountain and reached Amecameca the next day. The Italians soon joined us, having succeeded in reaching the Picacho del Frayle, a peak some 2,000 feet from the summit, when they were obliged to turn back, as one of them began to spit blood.

After some discussion, the majority of our party decided that it was impossible to reach the top, and that another effort was useless; but a few of us determined to make the trial. We immediately obtained some sulfate of lead with which we bathed our eyes. We also provided ourselves with green spectacles and warm clothing. The next evening found six of us, with about twenty-five infantry, encamped at the extreme limit of vegetation, some three miles in advance of our former camp at the *vacaría*.

Meanwhile, the remainder of the party had separated, one portion having returned to Mexico to give an account of our defeat, and the other portion having started for Cuernavaca to visit a celebrated cave in the vicinity, which would repay them for their disappointment in not getting to the summit of Popocatepetl.[8]

We left camp before 3 o'clock on the morning of the 11th [of April]. Our eyes were nearly well, our faces were still slightly swollen, and the skin had all peeled off, but we had several advantages over our first start, for we were some three miles further advanced, there was a prospect of a fair day, and we had a protection for our eyes and were warmly clad. We rode our mules some two miles, until the ascent became too great for them, when we sent them back to camp. We had provided ourselves with long poles with iron pikes on the ends, which we found to be invaluable. We passed over some three or four miles on a surface of black sand. This distance on our previous trial we had found covered with snow; it was now melted, and as the sand had absorbed the water and frozen, we got along without much difficulty.

We had reached an elevation of about two thousand feet above our camp by sunrise. The scene was then beautiful beyond description. The mountain cast a shadow which extended, not only across the whole valley to the horizon, but it reached beyond into the sky, and its outline was so detailedly defined that we could distinguish even the shadow cast by the smoke as it rose from the crater. As we advanced, our progress began to be impeded by the snow, and the atmosphere was so

Summit of Popocatepetl Volcano (photograph by Robert R. Miller)

rare that we breathed with great difficulty. As we reached the summit, the snow varied in depth from a few inches to three or four feet, and from five to ten steps were all that we could make without becoming exhausted. Our faces, and particularly our lips, were of a deep bluish-black color, and our heads ached intensely. Still, we succeeded in reaching the summit by half past ten. We were standing on the highest point of land in North America. Our first action after catching breath was to give three cheers and plant a small flag upon the summit.[9]

We next examined the crater; it was about five hundred feet in depth and some four or five hundred yards in diameter. The lip or mouth was an ellipse, being formed by having a plain oblique to the axis, with the highest point towards the west; the portion towards Puebla being, we thought, about two hundred feet lower than the opposite side. The walls were almost vertical, and a horizontal section would be nearly, if not quite, circular. The sides seemed to formed by three vertical cylinders, one within the other, the lowest being some two hundred feet where there was an irregular horizontal bench of a few yards in width, where it was intersected by the second cylinder, which rose some two hundred feet more, the third cylinder rising to the top of the cone. The sides of the crater poured out smoke from several places, some of them within a few yards from the top. Two large columns of smoke rose from the bottom, apparently from a large bed of sulphur. As some patches of snow were lying on the bottom, it was evident that little or no heat rose from the bowels below.

The view from our position was sublime beyond description, for we had one advantage which no party had ever enjoyed that had ever been here, it was a clear day. Some clouds were forming below us, but the snow [-peaked] mountain of Orizaba and the Nevado of Toluca were distinctly visible, rising like two large white rocks from the ocean. The whole country below us looked like a vast sea with slight undulations. Even Iztaccihuatl, which is some fifteen hundred or two thousand feet lower than the height on which we stood, appeared far below us.[10] Puebla, with its entire valley was to be seen. We could see far into the *tierra caliente.* Mexico [City], with her lakes, was to be seen somewhat indistinctly, as clouds were forming in that direction. After gratifying our curiosity about half an hour, we found it necessary to commence our descent as every one of the party was suffering with inflamation of the throat, nausea at the stomach, and violent headaches produced by the vapors of sulphur which rose from the crater.

We collected a few specimens of lava and commenced our descent. The change as we left this great elevation was apparent. As we reached the valley, all the sickly sensations left us, and when we reached our camp, which was at two o'clock, we felt perfectly well, with the exception of our headaches. The Indians would not believe us when we told them we had been to the summit. They examined our heads and said it was impossible, for no one could go there without having horns growing out of the top of their head, and as we had none, we had not been there. Our guides only went to the snow line; no persuasion or amount of money would induce them to go farther. One of our party, an ordnance soldier, got lost in descending the mountain and has not been heard of since.

Captain [James V.] Bomford, 8th Infantry; Lieutenant [Sterne H.] Fowler, 5th Infantry; Lieutenant [Richard H.] Anderson, 2nd Dragoons; Lieutenants Kirkham and Buckner, 6th Infantry; and Lieutenant Stone, Ordnance Corps, were the only ones of the twenty-five officers who attempted the ascent and succeeded.[11]

We reached Mexico [City] on the 14th, after an absence of twelve days, and found that everyone was ready to sympathize with us for our failure, but when the truth was made known, we were congratulated on every side. This is the first excursion to the top of any one of the four snow mountains in Mexico by any of our officers since the Army had been in the country, and the first by any Americans to the summit of the volcano of Popocatepetl. It was a remarkable coincidence that one year ago from the day and hour I was on the summit of this volcano, viz. on the 11th of April, 1847, I parted from my beloved wife in New Orleans. It was at half past ten o'clock in the morning; at this hour one year afterward, I was standing on the [fifth] highest point of land in North America.

LETTER, April 15, 1848. Tacubaya.

My own dear Kate:

It is nearly two weeks since I last wrote you. I was then just starting upon an expedition to Popocatepetl. I returned last evening, and now I sit down to give you an account of our excursion. [The account in this letter has been deleted because it is virtually identical to that in Kirkham's journal.] I enjoyed the excursion very much. One poor fellow got lost coming down, and we have not heard of him since.

Col. Loomis has not yet arrived, but we look for him daily. A mail has arrived since we were gone, but strange to say, I did not receive a single letter. Another one is due in three days; then I am sure I shall hear from you.

We hardly know what to think of getting out of the country. Peace stock remains about the same, but the Mexicans are such slow people, they take so much time. The yellow fever is prevailing quite extensive at Veracruz, and I am afraid we will not be able to get away until fall. Our sick have been sent off to Jalapa to be ready for a move if necessary. Colonel Sevier has not arrived; Mr. Clifford is here, but has done nothing. April 16th. Col. Sevier arrived last night. It is impossible to say what will be done, but the season is so far advanced that we are all afraid that we cannot with prudence think of leaving before fall. [12]

Oh my dearest wife, what patience is necessary to bear all this; we have been separated over a year! But I see no remedy. Can you wait a few months more? Be not afraid of any changes in me. I am sure my beloved one that no matter how long we may be apart, I shall love you with all the devotion, and with all the purity of heart that I did when I first whispered my tale of love to you on the 19th of July 1846.

Yes, I know my attachment is stronger now than it was then, for I did not know your worth then. But now, through all my joys and sorrows, I have had the sympathy of one whom I can trust; one who makes life itself dear to me. May My Heavenly Father ever smile on you and make you perfectly happy; all my prayers are for you. I need for myself nothing more. I am blessed with all that I could wish. I only desire to be more pure in heart and to again press my darling wife to my bosom. Everything else is granted me. Oh Kate, "Hope on, Hope ever," the future is before us full of joys and happiness. Never despond, but daily, yes hourly, enjoy the blessings which our Father bestows upon us.

Goodbye. God bless you. Give my love to all my dear friends and kiss the children for me. When you write to [relatives in] New Orleans, remember me kindly to our brother and sister Mary, not forgetting Vinny.[13]

Your ever affectionate husband, R. W. Kirkham

JOURNAL, April 17, 1848. Tacubaya.

My dear brother [-in-law] James [Mix] called on me today. He arrived day before yesterday from New Orleans and was only thirteen days on the road. I have been delighted with his visit, for he resembles my dearest wife so much, and his manners and actions are so much like hers that I can hardly keep my eyes off him.

JOURNAL, May 22, 1848. Tacubaya.

The commissioners left the city this morning for Querétaro [the temporary seat of the Mexican government], having received notification that the treaty had passed the [Mexican] lower house, and that they might come on and receive the exchange [of signatures]. We are all confident of soon being in the United States and again with those we love. There is hardly a doubt against the speedy peace. Arrangements are being made to move as soon as we shall hear of the ratification. General Smith leaves in a day or two for Veracruz to get transportation ready by the time the Army reaches the coast. Joy is seen on the countenances of all; many have been absent from their friends for nearly three years, some for two, and nearly all for more than one.

It is nearly fourteen months since I bid goodbye to my dear wife, but I hope in four or five weeks at farthest to meet her again.

JOURNAL, June 5, 1848. Mexico City.

National Palace, Mexico City. Today our brigade has moved from Tacubaya to this place. Colonel Clarke and myself are quartered in the palace with Major Shover's battery and two companies of the 6th Infantry.[14] The whole army has left for Veracruz, excepting one brigade of General Harney's division, which moves in the morning.

JOURNAL, June 11, 1848. Mexico City.

I visited today the Hospital of Jesus, an institution founded by Cortez and still in possession of his descendants. It has a full-length portrait of the Marquis and is the original of the many paintings and engravings which are to be found in this country.[15] I saw, in the church attached to the establishment, a room with the ceiling of carved cedar; the carving was in the Moorish style and was to me a great curiosity. It is probably like that described by Washington Irving in the Alhambra.[16] The carving was some six or eight inches in depth. In the same room I saw a table, the top of which is made of one entire piece of wood, and is seven feet two inches in diameter. The wood was also of cedar and is polished to resemble mahogany. The tree, I understand, grew at Tacubaya and was cut soon after the [Spanish] conquest.

JOURNAL, June 12, 1848. Ayotla.

Today the last of our army left the city of the Aztecs. Our division was formed in the grand plaza at 5 o'clock in the morning. At six, our flag flying on the national palace was saluted by thirty guns from Duncan's battery, and twenty-one from a Mexican battery. As our colors were lowered, the bands of the different regiments played "The Star-Spangled Banner." The Mexican flag was now hoisted and received the like salute from both batteries, and the Mexican national airs were now struck up. We then marched from the city, the Mexican national guards taking possession of the palace. There was no disturbance as we marched through the streets; on the contrary, the same people who actually stoned us when we entered the city now seemed sorry to have us go. Our march the first day was to Ayotla, where we encamped for the night. The whole division encamped together.

Journal, June 13, 1848. Río Frío.

Our march today has been a severe one, from Ayotla to Río Frío. It rained some two or three hours before we reached camp. Our brigade was in advance, and the leading regiment reached the Río at 3 o'clock. The rain was very cold, and we suffered exceedingly during the night. The other brigade did not reach camp until towards morning, and even then the 4th Infantry was not up.

Journal, June 15, 1848. Hacienda of San Bartolomé.

We marched today to the hacienda of San Bartolomé, distance some three or four miles beyond San Martín. We had a most delightful camp on a thick clean sward of grass. We were in camp by three o'clock.

Journal, June 16, 1848. Near Puebla.

We reached camp some three miles from Puebla by 10 o'clock in the morning. It is just thirteen months today since we entered this city on our way to the capital. We now have the snow mountains on our backs.

Journal, June 17, 1848. Amozoc.

We remained in camp yesterday, marched through Puebla this morning, and here we are in our old camp where we had our stampede with General Santa Anna in May a year ago. The rainy season is fairly upon us. It rains now every day regularly.

Journal, June 23, 1848. Near Jalapa.

We left Amozoc on the 18th and encamped at Ojo de Agua that night. The next day we reached Tepeyahualco. On the 20th we stopped at Perote. This place, with the castle, we turned over to the [Mexican] national guards. On the 21st we marched 20 miles to La Hoya and reached our camp, which is about three miles from Jalapa, early in the morning. We find encamped here Harney's division. There is some delay in embarking the troops at Veracruz for want of sufficient transports. We expect to remain here some eight or ten days before we leave. Our camp is comfortable, fine, open meadow, with a running stream through the encampment.

JOURNAL, July 9, 1848. Near Jalapa.

We have been in camp at this place more than a fortnight, and there is a prospect of our remaining here some time yet. On the 4th of July we had a dinner; the officers of the 6th [Regiment] invited the 8th, and the officers generally, I thought, enjoyed themselves.

Yesterday a party of us visited a village, which lies off the main road to the north some two or three miles, called Hilotepec in Indian, and in Spanish Jilotepec. It is one of the most beautiful little places I ever saw. The place is entirely cut off from the world, for it is at the very bottom of a deep dell, surrounded on all sides but towards the south by high hills. It is some hundred feet below Jalapa, and evidently is in the *tierra caliente* [hot country]. The object which took us there is a beautiful cascade which well paid us for our ride. The stream is rather small, but the water is perfectly clear, and at two leaps, bounds some one hundred and fifty feet into the valley. We spent an hour or two very pleasantly, then we returned with the *cura* [priest], who kindly accompanied us, and sat down to a dinner which he had prepared for us at his house. In the center of the village lies a high conical-shaped hill, on the summit of which is an old tower, now in ruins, which, covered as it was with vines, attracted our particular attention.

JOURNAL, July 13, 1848. Camp at the hacienda of Encero.

We left our camp at Jalapa yesterday and encamped here last night. The news from the coast is very favorable, and we expect to find transportation ready for us on our arrival at Veracruz.

JOURNAL, July 15, 1848. Steamship *Alabama* off Veracruz.

We arrived here this morning at 10 o'clock, being only three days from Jalapa. Our march from Plan del Río, some forty-six miles, was made without halting. We left Plan del Río on the morning of the 14th and made our march for the day, but soon after we were in camp at Paso de Ovejas, an express arrived from General Worth informing us that a steamer had arrived and was waiting us. So, tired as the regiment was, it was decided to strike our camp and resume our march at once. The moon shone bright, and we arrived at Veracruz pretty tired but in excellent spirits at the prospect of a comfortable passage in the *Alabama*. We found the *vómito* [yellow fever] had made its appearance, and it was time to be off. We are the first regiment of the division really ready to start. The 2nd and 3rd Regiments of Artillery are on board of ships and sail for New York. The 4th Infantry sail tomorrow on the British steamer *Great Western*.

JOURNAL, July 20, 1848. New Orleans.

We arrived last night in four days from Veracruz. We were at Jalapa a week ago. We had a delightful trip, no cases of *vómito* on board, which we expected would break out. I was seasick nearly all the time until we arrived at Balize [at the mouth of the Mississippi River].[17]

JOURNAL, July 21, 1848. Aboard [river] Steamer *Illinois*.

We are all on board a fine boat and expect to be in St. Louis in five days. The *New Orleans* came in from Veracruz a few minutes ago, and she had several cases of the *vómito* on her passage. Several men died. Oh what great cause for gratitude I have for the ten thousand blessings I have received from my Heavenly Father from the time I came into Mexico a year ago last April.

Epilogue

♣

WHEN THE MEXICAN WAR ENDED, Ralph Kirkham had been in the United States Army for ten years, counting his West Point service, and he was to remain in the army for another twenty-two years. Upon returning to New Orleans in midsummer of 1848, he was reunited with his wife Catherine. Together they journeyed to St. Louis, where he received a two-month furlough, which permitted the young couple to visit his family in Springfield, Massachusetts. There, he introduced "Kate" to his parents, brother, sisters, and other relatives.

Kirkham's postwar military duty stations spanned the western half of the United States. His first six years were split between two posts on the Mississippi River: Fort Snelling, Minnesota, and Jefferson Barracks, Missouri. Then, in November, 1854, he was transferred to the Pacific Coast, where he would spend the rest of his army career as a quartermaster. Traveling by steamship from New Orleans to Panama, Kirkham and his wife and two young daughters crossed the isthmus, and then they boarded another steamer for San Francisco, California, where they arrived in mid-March of 1855.[1] His first assignment in California was at Fort Tejon, which had been established the previous year as an outpost to protect travelers from Indians. Located about seventy-five miles north of Los Angeles, the fort was in a wooded pass beside the winding mountain stream known as Grapevine Creek. Here, while living with his family in a tent, Kirkham supervised the building of adobe barracks and officers' quarters.[2] At the end of 1856 he was promoted to the rank of captain.

In 1857, Kirkham was reassigned to San Francisco, where, except for part of one year, he served as quartermaster for the remaining thirteen years of his army career. He purchased a large home across the bay at Eighth and Oak streets in Oakland, California, where he and his wife raised four daughters: Leila, Julia, Maria ("May"), and Kate.[3] During a temporary assignment to Fort Walla Walla, Washington Territory, Captain Kirkham was twice cited for gallantry in the

Indian campaigns waged in August, 1858. One of his fellow officers later wrote: "Our quartermaster was Captain (now General) Ralph W. Kirkham, and he fully satisfied all the requirements of his office. Never did a man more completely escape notice by the perfection of his work than did General Kirkham in the campaign of 1858."[4]

When the American Civil War erupted in 1861, Kirkham volunteered to return to the East Coast for front-line duty, but he was ordered to remain in San Francisco as quartermaster. One of his important duties was forwarding gold to Washington, where it was used to purchase armaments. A number of Kirkham's West Point classmates actively participated in that momentous conflict. Of the fifty-six members of his class of 1842, five had been killed in the Mexican War, thirteen had died in the intervening years, and many had left army service. During the Civil War twelve of Kirkham's classmates were promoted or breveted to the rank of general in the Union forces, and ten members of the class of 1842 became generals in the army of the Confederate states.[5] Of course, other classmates served with lesser ranks. In 1863, Kirkham was promoted to major, and toward the end of the war he received the brevet ranks of lieutenant colonel, colonel, and brigadier general. Kirkham did not keep a journal or write an account of his activities in the Civil War.

Many of the men mentioned in Kirkham's Mexican War journal and letters had notable careers after that war. General Zachary Taylor's victories in northern Mexico had made him a hero at home and propelled him into the White House in 1849. Winfield Scott, who was commanding general of the United States Army for thirty years, was promoted to lieutenant general in 1852, the same year during which he was an unsuccessful candidate for the presidency. Franklin Pierce, a brigadier general of the U.S. Volunteers under Scott in Mexico, defeated his former commander in the presidential election of 1852 and became the fourteenth president. Ulysses S. Grant, who as a junior officer in Mexico began the climb of Popocatepetl with Lieutenant Kirkham, was promoted to lieutenant general during the Civil War, and he later served two terms as president of the United States.

Besides those officers who were nominated for, or became, president, several others whom Kirkham mentioned in his journal played prominent roles in American history. General William Worth commanded the Department of Texas immediately after the Mexican War, until he died there of cholera in 1849. The city of Fort Worth is named

Ralph W. Kirkham, c. 1870 (photograph, Oakland Museum, Oakland, Calif.)

for him. Generals Joseph Lane and John Quitman became U.S. senators; Cadwalader and Patterson were major generals in the Union army; and Twiggs, Pillow, and Johnson served as Confederate generals.

In 1870, after thirty-two years in the United States Army, General Kirkham resigned his commission and focused his interests toward business. An Oakland city directory for 1878 lists Kirkham's occupation as "capitalist." He was a founding director of the Union National Gold Bank, which later became the Union Savings Bank, and he developed some real estate in Oakland. Two of his brothers-in-law, Gustave and William Mix, were in the land title and real estate business in that city.[6] While eschewing political office, Kirkham was a civic leader who promoted hospitals and schools for his municipality.

One of Kirkham's associates in Oakland was Colonel John Coffee Hays, famed commander of the Texas Rangers during the Mexican War. "Jack" Hays moved to California in 1850 and two years later joined with four other men to purchase a huge tract of land which became the site of Oakland. Hays subsequently sold residential lots to Kirkham and hundreds of other settlers, and he donated land to burgeoning railroads and gaslight companies, as well as to schools, churches, parks, and the county seat. Hays served with Kirkham on the board of directors of several businesses, including the Union Savings Bank. In September, 1879, the two friends participated in the reception for former president Ulysses S. Grant, who visited Oakland, and the following year they were special guests at a banquet given by the Mexican War Veterans in honor of General William T. Sherman's visit.[7]

At his home in Oakland, General Kirkham amassed a personal library of more than two thousand volumes, most of them marked with his ex libris. A seventy-page manuscript inventory of his books, compiled in 1875, is in the California Historical Society. The catalogue is arranged alphabetically by author in twenty-two categories including ancient history, English literature, and military tactics.[8] A visitor to Kirkham's library in his Oakland home in 1878 said that it represented "the slow accumulation of a number of years in the hands of a book lover and reader." She described the collection and its setting as follows:

> General Kirkham's library is, in some respects, the most perfect in its interior arrangement and finish of any in the State. The room, though somewhat inadequate for the number of books, is a cosy family reading-

Kirkham's Oakland residence, 1887 (photograph, Torres Collection)

room, and is enlarged by the addition of a deep bay-window, affording ample light. The finish of the whole room is in solid black walnut; and the mantel, book-cases and bay-window arch, all of chaste architectural design, are heavily and richly carved. The bookcases are finished upon the walls, and occupy every available space. A large library table, with a full set of leather-covered furniture, complete the appointments of the room, and on either side of the curious clock finished in the mantel is a pair of bronzes.[9]

General Kirkham obtained some of his books, scrolls, and manuscripts during extensive travels in Europe and the Orient. In 1868–69 he and his family toured Europe for almost a year. The following year he and his daughter Leila accompanied former secretary of state William H. Seward on the first part of the statesman's trip around the world. In the autumn of 1870 they sailed from San Francisco to Yokohama aboard the steamship *China;* from there they went on to China before Kirkham and his daughter returned to California. In 1881 Kirkham took his sixteen-year-old daughter Kate on an extended tour of Europe. Her journal gives details and impressions of their visits to Belgium, France, Switzerland, Austria, Germany, Poland, Swe-

Ralph W. Kirkham's bookplate (Torres Collection)

den, and Russia. Four years later General Kirkham took his daughter Maria ("May") on a year-long trip to the European continent. The retired general also visited the Hawaiian Islands.[10]

Ralph Wilson Kirkham died at his home in Oakland on May 24, 1893, and his widow died four and a half years later on October 3, 1897. His obituary in the San Francisco *Call* estimated the estate at "more than $2,000,000," but a later edition of the newspaper said that the appraised value was $673,125.75.[11] The editor of another San Francisco newspaper eulogized the general in the following words:

> In these days of shoddy greatness it is pleasant to meet a true gentleman. Such was General R. W. Kirkham, who has just departed this life. As he walked the streets of Oakland in his unassuming way, as he performed his duties to the church of which he was a faithful officer and member, as he greeted his fellow-men of all classes with genuine courtesy, he left the impress of kindness and good-will to all; and few would have dreamed that this unassuming man had a remarkable record as a brave soldier on the battlefield. He was an able business man and has left an ample estate. Both the General and his good wife, who survives him, have long been known for their numerous charities and

many a needy household has been provided with the necessaries of life given by unknown hands and the bills paid by the General. . . . If more of our rich men followed in the footsteps of General Kirkham the world's poor would be happier and the rich would discover that their wealth was a blessing not only to themselves, but to their fellowmen.[12]

Ralph W. Kirkham and his wife Catherine left their mark on history in a number of ways. He was a founder and longtime officer of the Mountain View Cemetery Association, Oakland's principal cemetery. He donated the land for Saint John's Episcopal Church, of which he was a charter member and senior warden. Kirkham also gave five thousand dollars to the Oakland City Hospital and a large endowment to St. Luke's Hospital.[13] His wife was very active in church work and was a sponsor and the first president of Fabiola Hospital, established in 1876 as a medical facility "for the worthy, non-indigent poor."[14] Although there are no bronze plaques in Oakland or San Francisco honoring the Kirkham family, both cities have a Kirkham Street named for the general. Donated Kirkham items can be found in various places in San Francisco: his military sword is on display at the Presidio Army Museum, a church bell that he brought back from Mexico is in the Arboretum of Golden Gate Park, and some of his books, along with the catalogue of his Oakland library, are in the California Historical Society. Now, with the publication of his Mexican War journal, Kirkham shares another family treasure with the public.

Notes

INTRODUCTION

1. Recent scholarly books include Dana, *Monterrey Is Ours!*; Eisenhower, *So Far From God;* Johannsen, *To the Halls of the Montezumas;* Miller, *Shamrock and Sword;* Robinson, *The View from Chapultepec;* Sandweiss, Stewart, and Huseman, *Eyewitness to War;* and Vásquez and Meyer, *The United States and Mexico.*

2. Published journals and diaries listed in Tutorow, *The Mexican-American War,* pp. 265–69; and Bauer, *The Mexican War,* pp. 410–19. Also see: McWhiney and McWhiney, *To Mexico With Taylor and Scott.*

3. *Appleton's Cyclopedia of American Biography,* 3:555; Kirkham family documents and papers in possession of Sarah Torres, Kentfield, Calif.

4. Frisch, *Town Into City,* p. 15.

5. Kirkham's early schooling in his obituary in the Springfield, Mass. *Republican,* May 25 and 28, 1893.

6. Cadet life in Dupuy, *Where They Have Trod,* pp. 23, 28, and 68; and Ambrose, *Duty, Honor, Country,* pp. 163–64.

7. As of 1990, the original small notebook was in the possession of Kirkham's great-granddaughter, Sarah Torres.

8. Fleming, *West Point,* p. 112.

9. Prucha, *A Guide to the Military Forts of the United States,* pp. 76, 112–13.

10. Ralph W. Kirkham to Catherine M. Kirkham, letter, Puebla, Mexico, June 8, 1847, Torres Collection.

11. Her parents were Elija Mix and Maria Cooper Mix; her brothers were named William A., Theodore, James, Edwin C., Alfred D., and Gustave L.; her married sister, Sophie Hart, lived in Alton, Ill. James and William Mix served as soldiers in the Mexican War.

12. See R. W. Kirkham's letter dated Nov. 10, 1847, this volume.

13. Singletary, *The Mexican War,* pp. 14–15; Pletcher, *The Diplomacy of Annexation,* pp. 64–69; and Horsman, *Race and Manifest Destiny,* pp. 208–20.

14. Pletcher, *The Diplomacy of Annexation,* pp. 94–100, 307–308; Sears, *John Slidell,* ch. 3; and Bauer, *The Mexican War,* p. 24.

15. Brack, *Mexico Views Manifest Destiny,* p. 110; Richardson, *Texas,* pp. 100, 106–23.

16. Polk, *The Diary of a President,* pp. 65–66, 106; Sellers, *James K. Polk,*

p. 407; Stenberg, "The Failure of Polk's Mexican War Intrigues," pp. 35–68.

17. Smith, *The War with Mexico,* pp. 139–40; Bauer, *The Mexican War,* p. 37; and Weems, *To Conquer a Peace,* p. 97.

18. Smith, *War with Mexico,* p. 148; Bauer, *The Mexican War,* pp. 39–40, 46–48; and Weems, *To Conquer a Peace,* p. 109.

19. Smith, *War with Mexico,* pp. 149–50; Richardson, *Messages and Papers of the Presidents,* 4:442; *Diario del Gobierno del la República mexicana* (Mexico City), July 7, 1846.

20. Frederick Merk, "Dissent in the Mexican War," in Morison, Merk, and Freidel, *Dissent in Three American Wars,* pp. 33–63; Johannsen, *To the Halls of the Montezumas,* pp. 8, 10–11.

21. In all, some 30,954 regular troops and officers of the United States Army and 73,776 militiamen and U.S. Volunteers, plus 7,500 sailors and marines served in Mexico during those two wartime years. Heitman, *Historical Register and Dictionary of the United States Army,* 2:282.

CHAPTER ONE

1. Major Burton Randall, a surgeon; Charles P. Deyerle, assistant surgeon; Second Lieutenant Anderson D. Nelson, Sixth Infantry.

2. Dr. McCormick was the house doctor for the St. Charles Hotel, New Orleans.

3. Junior army officers were permitted one servant, majors and colonels two, brigadier generals three. See Robert E. May, "Invisible Men: Blacks and the U.S. Army in the Mexican War," *The Historian* 49 (Aug., 1987): 466.

4. The "castle" was the fortified small island of San Juan de Ulúa, about one thousand yards offshore.

5. George Wilkins Kendall, cofounder of the New Orleans *Picayune,* was the first modern war correspondent and the most widely known reporter in the United States in his day. Copeland, *Kendall of the Picayune,* p. 150. Major General Winfield Scott (1786-1866) had been an officer in the army since 1808; in 1841 he became general in chief of the army, and in 1846 he was named head of the force that was to invade Mexico near Veracruz. Spiller, *Dictionary of American Military Biography,* 3:972–75. Antonio López de Santa Anna (1794–1876), who became a lieutenant in the army at age sixteen, subsequently rose to the rank of general and was involved in numerous political and military revolts. In Apr., 1847, he held the rank of major general and had been named president of his nation for the ninth time. *Enciclopedia de México,* s.v. "López de Santa Anna, Antonio."

6. American losses totaled 431, of whom 63 were killed. General Scott's report of Apr. 23, 1847, in 30th U.S. Cong., 1st Sess., *Senate Exec. Doc. No. 1,* p. 274. Mexican losses stated as 1,500 killed, wounded, and dispersed, plus 3,700 who surrendered. Carlos María de Bustamante, *El nuevo Bernal Díaz*

del Castillo, o sea, historia de la invasión de los Anglo-Americanos a México, 2:190.

7. First Lieutenant Napoleon J. Dana, Seventh Infantry; he survived, see journal entry of Apr. 29, 1846, this volume.

8. The hacienda of Manga de Clavo, a favorite of Santa Anna, encompassed 220,000 acres. Jones, *Santa Anna,* p. 95.

9. William J. Worth, who had been in the army since 1813, had fought in northern Mexico, where he received a brevet promotion to major general. He was commander of the first division of the force under General Scott. Wallace, *General William Jenkins Worth.* Major General Zachary Taylor had been in the army for thirty-seven years. His battle victories in northern Mexico made him a hero and later contributed to his election as president. Bauer, *Zachary Taylor;* Spiller, *Dictionary of American Military Biography,* 3:1093–96.

10. David E. Twiggs had received a brevet commission as major general after the Battle of Monterrey, Mexico, in Sept., 1846. He was commander of the second division of the army under General Scott. Spiller, *Dictionary of American Military Biography,* 3:1119–22. John Q. Quitman, a brigadier general of U.S. Volunteers, had won distinction and brevet rank of major general at the Battle of Monterrey. He fought under General Scott at Veracruz and later became military governor of Mexico City during the American occupation. May, *John A. Quitman.*

11. The hacienda of El Encerro embraced 88,000 acres. Jones, *Santa Anna,* p. 95.

12. Colonel Newman S. Clarke had commanded the Sixth Infantry Regiment since June 29, 1846. Companies G and I of that regiment remained in the United States throughout the War.

13. The fortress of San Carlos de Perote was constructed by the Spaniards between 1770 and 1774 to protect the shipments of silver. It was quadrangular and surrounded by a moat. McGrath and Hawkins, "Perote Fort," pp. 340–45.

14. Rev. John McCarty, an Episcopalian who before the war had a church in Syracuse, N.Y. (Davis, *Autobiography,* p. 186); Second Lieutenant William T. Burwell, Fifth Infantry; Captain Albermarle Cady, Sixth Infantry; and First Lieutenant Edward H. Fitzgerald, Sixth Infantry.

15. Mexican records give a cost of 700,000 pesos. *Enciclopedia de México,* s.v. "Fortificaciones."

16. Guadalupe Victoria (1786–1843), whose real name was Manuel Félix Fernández, was a Mexican Independence war hero and first president of Mexico; General Juan Nepomuceno Almonte (1802–1869) was a military officer, diplomat, and erstwhile cabinet official.

17. Lancers were light cavalry armed with lances, or long spears, varying from eight to eleven feet in length.

18. Dragoons were mounted infantrymen who normally dismounted before fighting.

CHAPTER TWO

1. The bishop was Francisco Pablo Vázquez Vizcaíno.

2. Puebla's stunning Cathedral of the Immaculate Conception, constructed of blue-gray basalt stone, was completed in the seventeenth century. Toussaint, *La catedral y las iglesias de Puebla,* pp. 58–60.

3. Colonel William Selby Harney, Second Dragoons, was the chief cavalryman under General Scott.

4. Francis L. Hawks, D.D., rector of Christ Church from 1845–49.

5. Second Lieutenant Franklin W. Flint, Sixth Infantry, who graduated from West Point in 1841, one year before Kirkham.

6. A Mexican peso, then worth about one U.S. dollar, was divided into eight reales.

7. General Nicolás Bravo (1786–1854) had been a Mexican Independence war hero, twice interim president of Mexico, and in the summer of 1847 was one of the defenders of Mexico City.

8. William A. Mix (1825–90) was an enlisted soldier in the Mexican War. Obituary in Oakland, Calif. *Enquirer,* Jan. 6, 1890.

9. More than eighty churches and convents are described in Toussaint, *La catedral y las iglesias de Puebla.*

10. Corpus Christi (Body of Christ) is the feast of the Blessed Sacrament celebrated on the Thursday following the first Sunday after Pentecost. Broderick, *Concise Catholic Dictionary.*

11. John B. Kirkham (1791–1857); Albert H. Kirkham (1825–1908); Frances M. Kirkham (1823–92), who married James Kirkham; and Jeanette S. Kirkham (1819–55), who married Thomas Wright. Colonel Gustavus Loomis commanded the Sixth Infantry Regiment after Jan. 5, 1846; Kirkham had served under him at Fort Towson. Loomis was married to Catherine Mix Kirkham's aunt Julia; see letter dated June 8, 1847, this volume. Ogden was Captain Edmund A. Ogden, Eighth Infantry. Alfred Mix lived in New Orleans, La.

12. Colonel Ethan Allen Hitchcock, adjutant to General Scott and inspector general. Spiller, *Dictionary of American Military Biography,* 2:475–78.

13. General Mariano Arista (1802–55), career officer and commander of the Army of the North, became president of Mexico in 1851; General Pedro de Ampudia (1803–68), longtime military commander in northern Mexico, had fought against General Taylor.

14. Smith was Brevet Lieutenant Colonel Charles F. Smith, First Artillery.

15. This was Captain Charles S. Lovell, Sixth Infantry.

16. Brevet Colonel Thomas Childs, First Artillery.

17. Major General Gideon J. Pillow, a former law partner of President James Polk, commanded the U.S. Volunteers. Spiller, *Dictionary of American Military Biography,* 2:861–65. Brigadier General George Cadwalader, commander of the Pennsylvania Volunteers.

18. The officers mentioned were Major Carlos A. Waite, Eighth Infantry; Major Charles S. Tripler, surgeon; Captain Francis Taylor, First Artillery; Captain Joseph R. Smith, Second Infantry; Captain James W. Penrose, Second Infantry; First Lieutenant Delozier Davidson, Second Infantry; Captain Charles Hanson, Seventh Infantry; First Lieutenant Andrew J. Lindsay, Mounted Rifles; Lieutenant Charles P. Stone, Ordnance; First Lieutenant William A. Nichols, Second Artillery; First Lieutenant Samuel S. Anderson, Second Artillery; Lieutenant James G. Martin, First Artillery; Captain Benjamin S. Roberts, Mounted Rifles.

19. The pyramid of Cholula is the largest in volume of any in the Americas and is larger than the Egyptian pyramid of Cheops at Giza. At the time of the Spanish Conquest the city and its suburbs contained forty thousand houses. Hunter, *Guide to Ancient Mexican Ruins,* p. 59. The "ancient church" is the church of Nuestra Señora de los Remedios.

20. Brigadier General Franklin Pierce, former congressman and senator, who later became fourteenth U.S. president.

21. The Mexican Spy Company, composed of two hundred former guerrilla fighters and bandits, operated under Colonel Ethan A. Hitchcock. Hitchcock, *Fifty Years in Camp and Field,* pp. 259, 263–65.

22. This was Major Samuel Woods, Sixth Infantry. In 1856 he married Kirkham's sister, Jane Gray Kirkham.

CHAPTER THREE

1. The volcanic peak, also known as Citlaltepetl, is in Veracruz state; at 18,700 feet, it is Mexico's highest point.

2. There were five interconnected lakes named: Zumpango, Xaltocan, Texcoco, Xochimilco, and Chalco (some of the lakes have since dried up).

3. El Peñón was a hilltop fortress east of Mexico City.

4. The officers mentioned were Brevet Lieutenant Colonel James Duncan, Second Artillery; and First Lieutenant Charles S. Hamilton, Fifth Infantry.

5. A short armistice was arranged during which negotiations for peace would be pursued.

6. Captain Seth Thornton, Second Dragoons. His capture on the Rio Grande in Apr., 1846 was one pretext for the American declaration of war.

7. Mexicans call this the Battle of Padierna, from a nearby ranch of that name. The officers mentioned were First Lieutenant John P. Johnstone, First

Artillery; Second Lieutenant Thomas Easley, Second Infantry; Captain James W. Anderson, Second Infantry; Captain Joseph R. Smith, Second Infantry; Captain Martin J. Burke, First Artillery; Captain Erastus A. Capron, First Artillery; and Second Lieutenant Satterlee Hoffman, First Artillery.

8. The other "fort" was the fortified convent and church of Churubusco, where Major General Manuel Rincón had about fourteen hundred troops and seven artillery pieces.

9. The wounded officers were Major Benjamin L. Bonneville; Captain William Hoffman; First Lieutenant Thomas Hendrickson; Second Lieutenant Simon B. Buckner; and First Lieutenant John D. Bacon, all of the Sixth Infantry.

10. Escopets are carbines or short rifles.

11. The officers mentioned were Captain Philip Kearny, First Dragoons; Brevet First Lieutenant Lorimer Graham, Tenth Infantry; and Captain Andrew T. McReynolds, Third Dragoons.

12. First Lieutenant Joseph F. Irons, First Artillery; First Lieutenant James G. Martin, First Artillery.

13. These were members of the San Patricio Battalion of the Mexican army. Miller, *Shamrock and Sword,* pp. 88–89.

14. The Texan raiders had been captured near Mier, Tamaulipas, in Dec., 1842. Green, *Journal of the Texian Expedition Against Mier,* p. 107.

15. Private John Riley, who defected on the Rio Grande on Apr. 12, 1846, before war was declared, was not hanged; but he was whipped, branded with a *D* for deserter, and imprisoned for the duration of the war. Miller, *Shamrock and Sword,* p. 102.

16. McIntosh was Brevet Colonel James S. McIntosh, Fifth Infantry.

17. What the Americans thought was a foundry was in reality an old stone flour mill. The officers named were Major George Wright, Eighth Infantry; and Lieutenant Colonel John Garland, Fourth Infantry.

18. Colonel Martin Scott; Captain Moses E. Merrill; and Lieutenant Erastus B. Strong, all of the Fifth Infantry.

19. This was the bloodiest battle of the war: American casualties totaled 799 out of 3,447 engaged, about 23 percent; Mexican losses were perhaps 2,000 killed and wounded, 700 prisoners, and an indefinite number dispersed. Smith, *The War with Mexico,* 2:140–47, 403.

20. This was First Lieutenant William Armstrong, Second Artillery.

21. The officers named here were Captain William H. Walker, Captain Albermarle Cady, and Lieutenant Rudolph F. Ernst, all of the Sixth Infantry; Brevet Captain George W. Ayers, Third Artillery; and First Lieutenant Joseph F. Farry, Third Artillery.

22. The Mexican generals were General Antonio León (1794-1847) and General Lucas Balderas (1797-1847).

23. This was Colonel and Brevet Brigadier General Bennet Riley, Second Infantry.

24. Burbank and Smith were First Lieutenant John G. Burbank, Eighth Infantry; and Captain Ephraim Kirby Smith, Fifth Infantry.

25. Chapultepec Castle was on a hill dominating several approaches to Mexico City. Formerly a viceregal palace, it later became the Colegio Militar, and in Sept., 1847, was defended by nine hundred soldiers and forty-seven cadets.

26. American reports indicate that an attacking soldier cut the fuse hoses early in the battle.

27. Captain Peter V. Hagner, Ordnance.

28. Mariano Riva Palacio (1803–80) was a congressman and cabinet member.

Chapter Four

1. American casualties were 862; Mexican losses were estimated at three times that, including 823 men taken prisoner. Four of the teen-aged cadets were wounded in the battle, 37 were taken prisoner, and 6 died, one of them reputedly having wrapped himself in the national flag and hurled himself over the wall rather than surrender. Smith, *The War with Mexico;* 2:405–11.

2. Santa Anna was in the suburb of Guadalupe Hidalgo, where he split his army; he sent part of the forces to the city of Querétaro, where a refugee government was to be erected, and part went with him toward Puebla.

3. John Hill, the youngest of the Texans captured, was adopted by Santa Anna. Green, *Journal of the Texian Expedition,* p. 445. T. James Baygally was an English resident of Mexico City and professor in the Academia Nacional de Bellas Artes there.

4. The large bronze statue of Charles IV was designed by Manuel Tolsá; today it is located in front of the Museo Nacional de Arte.

5. His acquaintance was Miss Baygally, daughter of the English professor of art, T. J. Baygally.

6. The officers who died were First Lieutenant John D. Bacon and Second Lieutenant George T. Shackleford, both of the Sixth Infantry; and Dr. William Roberts, assistant surgeon.

7. Between 1832 and 1835 Captain Bonneville, with 107 volunteers from his regiment, made a semiofficial exploration of the Rocky Mountains and beyond.

8. Brevet is a commission promoting a military officer in rank without an increase in pay; it is generally awarded for gallantry in action. Although an honorary rank, it could determine command arrangements or order of seniority, and thus could affect assignments.

9. Woods was then in the Fifteenth Infantry, but previously he had been in the Sixth Infantry, Kirkham's regiment.

10. Patterson was Major General Robert Patterson of the U.S. Volunteers.

11. Nicholas Trist, chief clerk of the State Department, was sent to Mexico to negotiate peace; although recalled in Nov., 1847, he stayed and signed the Treaty of Guadalupe Hidalgo on Feb. 2, 1848, which was later accepted by both governments.

12. General Andrés Terrés (1777–1850), a career Mexican officer.

13. Smith was Brigadier General Persifor F. Smith of the U.S. Volunteers.

14. The reference is to First Lieutenant Franklin Flint, Sixth Infantry, who graduated from West Point in 1841, one year before Kirkham.

15. Benjamin K. Hart, M.D., was married to Kirkham's wife's sister, Sophie.

16. *The Cloth of Gold* was a drama in three acts; *The Grumbler* was published in New York in 1844.

17. She was the wife of John O'Sullivan, a merchant-tailor.

18. These officers were accused of writing slanted accounts, later published in the United States, of the battles near Mexico City. On Jan. 13, 1848, the secretary of war ordered their release. There is a good summary in Eisenhower, *So Far from God,* pp. 352–55, 364.

19. See ibid. Eisenhower maintains that Worth was technically innocent.

20. The *noche triste,* or sad night, was on June 30, 1520, when Hernán Cortés and his Spanish conquistadors fled Tenochtitlán, the Aztec capital. Captain Alvarado was Pedro de Alvarado.

21. The chapel of Our Lady of Remedies is on the hill of Toltepec, where, according to legend, the Virgin appeared to the Spanish army to give it courage.

22. Major General Gabriel Valencia (1799–1848) at that time commanded the Army of the North.

23. Brigadier General Joseph Lane's U.S. Volunteer troops were transferred from Taylor's forces to Scott's; they arrived in Veracruz in Sept., 1847, and then marched to the aid of Puebla, which was under siege.

24. Brigadier General Caleb Cushing's brigade had been transferred from General Taylor's force to Scott's army.

25. Major General William O. Butler, First Division of U.S. Volunteers.

26. The monastery and church of San Fernando, located about three blocks northwest of the Alameda, was built in the eighteenth century; it had an adjacent cemetery.

27. Lieutenant Colonel Charles K. Johnson, Louisiana Volunteers.

28. Laidley was First Lieutenant Theodore T. Laidley, Ordnance, a West Point classmate of Kirkham.

29. Señor Pizarro probably was Mexican rather than Spanish; Kirkham usually referred to all Mexican civilians as Spanish.

30. These were the silver mines of Pachuca, located fifty miles north of Mexico City.

CHAPTER FIVE

1. Toluca's elevation is 8,700 feet above the sea.

2. Jeanette S. Kirkham (1819–55) married Judge Thomas Wright.

3. The officers were Captain Thomas L. Alexander, Lieutenant Winfield S. Hancock, and Lieutenant Lewis A. Armistead, all Sixth Infantry. The "Snow Mountain" was Nevado de Toluca, which is 14,900 feet above sea level.

4. Major General Juan Alvarez (1790–1867) was a Mexican Independence hero and military chief of the Division of the South; in 1847 he was one of the defenders of Mexico City.

5. General Butler replaced the dismissed General Scott on Feb. 19; Generals Pillow and Worth and Colonel Duncan were released from arrest by order of the secretary of war, and a court of inquiry was appointed to investigate the dispute between them and General Scott. A regiment of Voltigeurs (light infantry) was organized by Act of Feb. 11, 1847. Heitman, *Historical Register,* 1:143.

6. John Bowdler (1783–1823), *Select Pieces in Verse and Prose.*

7. The Treaty of Guadalupe Hidalgo was signed on Feb. 2, 1848, and ratified by the U.S. Senate.

8. Lieutenant U. S. Grant was among those who turned back from the climb. Ulysses S. Grant, *Personal Memoirs,* 1:180–81.

9. Popocatepetl is actually the second-highest point in Mexico, after Orizaba, and the fifth-highest in North America, being surpassed also by McKinley, Logan, and St. Elias.

10. It is actually only 544 feet lower.

11. Anderson, Buckner, or Stone may have been the author of "A Visit to Popocatepetl," *Putnam's Monthly Magazine* 1 (Apr., 1853): 408–16. Grant, *Personal Memoirs,* 1:184.

12. Colonel Ambrose Sevier and Nathan Clifford were American peace commissioners.

13. This probably refers to Catherine's brother Edwin C. Mix and his wife Mary, who lived in New Orleans. Vinny may have been their servant.

14. Brevet Major William H. Shover, Third Artillery.

15. For service to the crown, Cortés was knighted as Marquis of the Valley of Oaxaca.

16. The reference is to *Tales of the Alhambra,* written in 1829 when Irving resided in the Alhambra palace in Granada, Spain.

17. Balize, a pilot site about ninety miles southeast of New Orleans, disappeared about 1900; it is shown on older maps and appears in *Lippincott's Gazeteer of the World.*

EPILOGUE

1. California State Library, Sacramento, Pioneer Card File, "Ralph Wilson Kirkham"; R. W. Kirkham's "Notebook" gives arrival date of Mar. 15, 1855.

2. *Appleton's Cyclopedia,* 3:555. Fort Tejon was abandoned in 1864; the site is now a California State Historical Park and contains some of the original adobe buildings. Hoover, Rensch, and Rensch, *Historic Spots in California,* p. 100.

3. Mary Leila Kirkham (1849–1904) married David Boyle Blair, and her second husband was Walter Yarde-Buller; Julia Edith Kirkham (1850–74) married Major Murray Davis; Maria Cooper Kirkham (1858–1921) married James De Forrest Safford; Kate Virginia Kirkham (1863–1946) married Peter Lansing Wheeler, M.D.

4. Keyes, *From West Point to California,* pp. 60–61. Kirkham's citations in Prosch, "The Indian War of 1858," pp. 239–40.

5. *Register of Graduates of the U.S. Military Academy,* pp. 228–30.

6. Langley, *Directory of the City of Oakland,* 1878–79, 1879–80.

7. Greer, *Colonel Jack Hays,* pp. 254–55, 283–84, 308, 343, 345, 352, 356, and 361–62. San Francisco *Call,* Sept. 15, 1880.

8. The catalogue of his library is MS 1197, California Historical Society, San Francisco.

9. Flora H. Apponyi [Loughead], *The Libraries of California,* p. 141.

10. *Appelton's Cyclopedia,* 3:555.

11. San Francisco *Call,* May 25, 1893 and Oct. 28, 1893.

12. San Francisco *Bulletin,* May 25, 1893.

13. Langley, *Directory of the City of Oakland,* 1878–79; Joseph E. Baker, *Past and Present of Alameda County,* pp. 362, 366. Obituaries of General Ralph W. Kirkham, Oakland, Calif. *Times,* May 25, 1893; San Francisco *Bulletin,* May 25, 1893; Springfield, Mass. *Republican,* May 26, 1893.

14. Obituary of Catherine Kirkham, San Francisco *Call,* Oct. 4, 1897. Originally known as the Oakland Homeopathic Hospital and Dispensary, the name was later changed to Fabiola in honor of the fourth-century Roman matron who founded a hospital for the sick poor. Bagwell, *Oakland,* pp. 134–35.

Bibliography

MANUSCRIPTS

California Historical Society, San Francisco
  MS 1197, "Catalogue of Ralph W. Kirkham's Library, 1875"
California State Library, Sacramento
  Pioneer Card File, "Ralph Wilson Kirkham"
Torres Collection, Kentfield, California
  Ralph W. Kirkham's Bookplate
  Ralph W. Kirkham's Mexican War Journal
  Ralph W. Kirkham's West Point Notebook
  Kate V. Kirkham's European Journal

NEWSPAPERS

Mexico City, *Diario del Gobierno de la República mexicana*
Oakland, California, *Enquirer*
Oakland, California, *Times*
San Francisco, California, *Call*
San Francisco, California, *Bulletin*
Springfield, Massachusetts, *Republican*

BOOKS AND MONOGRAPHS

Agnew, Brad. *Fort Gibson: Terminal on the Trail of Tears.* Norman: University of Oklahoma Press, 1980.

Alcaraz, Ramón, et al., eds. *Apuntes para la historia de la guerra entre México y los Estados Unidos.* Mexico: Tip. de M. Payno, 1848.

Ambrose, Stephen E. *Duty, Honor, Country: A History of West Point.* Baltimore, Md.: Johns Hopkins University Press, 1966.

Anderson, Robert. *An Artillery Officer in the Mexican War, 1846–47; Letters of Robert Anderson, Captain 3rd Artillery.* New York: G. P. Putnam's Sons, 1911.

Appleton's Cyclopedia of American Biography. New York: D. Appleton and Co., 1887. Vol. 3, "Kirkham, Ralph Wilson."

Babcock, Elkanah. *A War History of the Sixth U.S. Infantry from 1798 to 1903.* Kansas City: Hudson-Kemberly Publishing Co., 1903.

Bagwell, Beth. *Oakland: The Story of A City.* Novato, Calif.: Presidio Press, 1982.

Baker, Joseph Eugene. *Past and Present of Alameda County, Calilfornia.* 2 vols. Chicago, Ill.: Clarke, 1914.

Balbontín, Manuel. *La invasión americana, 1846 a 1847; apuntes del subteniente de artillería.* Mexico: Gonzalo A. Esteva, 1883.

Bauer, K. Jack. *The Mexican War, 1846–48.* New York: Macmillan, 1974.

———. *Zachary Taylor: Soldier, Planter, Statesman of the Old Southwest.* Baton Rouge: Louisiana State University Press, 1985.

Beauregard, Pierre G. *With Beauregard in Mexico: The Mexican War Reminiscences of P. G. T. Beauregard.* Ed. T. Harry Williams. Reprint, New York: Da Capo Press, 1969.

Brack, Gene M. *Mexico Views Manifest Destiny, 1821–1846: An Essay on the Origins of the Mexican War.* Albuquerque: University of New Mexico Press, 1975.

Broderick, Robert C., ed. *Concise Catholic Dictionary.* St. Paul, Minn.: Catechetical Guild Educational Society, 1944.

Bustamante, Carlos María de. *El nuevo Bernal Díaz del Castillo, o sea, historia de la invasión de los anglo-americanos a México.* 2 vols. in 1. Mexico: V. García Torres, 1847.

Castillo Negrete, Emilio del. *Invasión de los Norte Americanos en México.* 6 vols. Mexico: Imprenta del editor, 1890–91.

Connor, Seymour V., and Odie B. Faulk. *North America Divided: The Mexican War, 1846–1848.* New York: Oxford University Press, 1971.

Copeland, Fayette. *Kendall of the Picayune.* Norman: University of Oklahoma Press, 1943.

Dana, Napoleon J. *Monterrey Is Ours! The Mexican War Letters of Lt. Dana, 1845–1847.* Ed. Robert H. Ferrell. Lexington: University Press of Kentucky, 1990.

Davis, George T. M. *Autobiography of the Late Col. Geo. T. M. Davis, Captain and Aid-de-Camp Scott's Army of Invasion (Mexico).* New York: Jenkins and McCowan, 1891.

Diccionario Porrúa de historia, biografía y geografía de México. 3 vols. Mexico: Editorial Porrúa, 1986. S.v. "Popocatepetl."

Dupuy, R. Ernest. *Where They Have Trod: The West Point Tradition in American Life.* New York: Frederick A. Stokes Co., 1940.

Eisenhower, John S. *So Far from God: The U.S. War with Mexico, 1846–1848.* New York: Random House, 1989.

Enciclopedia de México. 1978 ed. S.v. "Fortificaciones"; "Guerra de E.U. a México"; "López de Santa Anna, Antonio."

Fleming, Thomas J. *West Point: The Men and Times of the United States Military Academy.* New York: William Morrow and Co., 1969.

Frisch, Michael H. *Town Into City: Springfield, Massachusetts, and the Meaning of Community, 1840–1880.* Cambridge, Mass.: Harvard University Press, 1972.

Grant, Ulysses S. *Personal Memoirs.* 2 vols. New York: C. L. Webster and Co., 1885–86.

Green, Thomas J. *Journal of the Texian Expedition Against Mier.* New York: Harper and Bros., 1845.

Greer, James K. *Colonel Jack Hays; Texas Frontier Leader and California Builder.* 2nd ed. College Station: Texas A&M University Press, 1987.

Heitman, Francis B. *Historical Register and Dictionary of the United States Army, from Its Organization, September 29, 1789, to March 2, 1903.* 2 vols. Washington, D.C.: Government Printing Office, 1903.

Hitchcock, Ethan A. *Fifty Years in Camp and Field: Diary of Major-General Ethan Allen Hitchcock, U.S.A.* Ed. W. A. Croffut. New York: G. P. Putnam's Sons, 1909.

Hoover, Mildred B., Hero E. Rensch, and Ethel G. Rensch. *Historic Spots in California.* Stanford, Calif.: Stanford University Press, 1948.

Horsman, Reginald. *Race and Manifest Destiny: The Origins of American Racial Anglo-Saxonism.* Cambridge, Mass.: Harvard University Press, 1981.

Hunter, C. Bruce. *A Guide to Ancient Mexican Ruins.* Norman: University of Oklahoma Press, 1977.

Johannsen, Robert W. *To the Halls of the Montezumas: The Mexican War in the American Imagination.* New York: Oxford University Press, 1985.

Jones, Oakah L., Jr. *Santa Anna.* New York: Twayne Publishers, 1968.

Keyes, Erasmus D. *From West Point to California.* Oakland, Calif.: Biobooks, 1950.

Langley, Henry G., comp. *A Directory of the City of Oakland and Its Environs.* Oakland, Calif.: Henry G. Langley, 1878–79, 1979–80.

Lippincott's Gazeteer of the World. Philadelphia, Pa.: J. B. Lippincott and Co., 1880.

[Loughead], Flora H. Apponyi. *The Libraries of California: Containing Descriptions of the Principal Private and Public Libraries Throughout the State.* San Francisco, Calif.: A. L. Bancroft and Co., 1878.

McClellan, George B. *The Mexican War Diary of George B. McClellan.* Ed. William S. Myers. Princeton, N.J.: Princeton University Press, 1917.

McGrath, J. J., and Walace Hawkins. "Perote Fort—Where Texans Were Imprisoned," *Southwestern Historical Quarterly* 48 (1943–44): 340–45.

McWhiney, Grady, and Sue McWhiney, comps. *To Mexico with Taylor and Scott, 1845–1847.* Waltham, Mass.: Blaisdell, 1969.

May, Robert E. "Invisible Men: Blacks and the U.S. Army in the Mexican War," *The Historian* 49 (Aug., 1987): 463–77.

———. *John A. Quitman: Old South Crusader.* Baton Rouge: Louisiana State University Press, 1985.

Miller, Robert Ryal. *Mexico: A History.* Norman: University of Oklahoma Press, 1985.

————. *Shamrock and Sword: The Saint Patrick's Battalion in the U.S.-Mexican War.* Norman: University of Oklahoma Press, 1989.

Morison, Samuel E., Frederick Merk, and Frank Freidel. *Dissent in Three American Wars.* Cambridge, Mass.: Harvard University Press, 1970.

Peck, John J. *The Sign of the Eagle; A View of Mexico—1830 to 1855.* Ed. Richard Pourade. San Diego, Calif.: Union-Tribune Publishing Co., 1970.

Pletcher, David M. *The Diplomacy of Annexation: Texas, Oregon, and the Mexican War.* Columbia: University of Missouri Press, 1973.

Polk, James K. *Polk: The Diary of a President.* Ed. Allan Nevins. London, New York, and Toronto: Longmans, Green and Co., 1929.

Prosch, Thomas W. "The Indian War of 1858," *Washington Historical Quarterly* 2 (1908): 237–40.

Prucha, Francis P. *A Guide to the Military Forts of the United States, 1789–1895.* Madison: State Historical Society of Wisconsin, 1964.

Register of Graduates of the U.S. Military Academy. Ed. Charles N. Branham. West Point: West Point Alumni Association, 1965. "Class of 1842," pp. 228–30.

Richardson, James D., ed. *A Compilation of the Messages and Papers of the Presidents, 1789–1897.* 10 vols. Washington, D.C.: Government Printing Office, 1896–99. S.v. "Polk's War Message to Congress," 4:437–43.

Richardson, Rupert N. *Texas: The Lone Star State.* Englewood, Cliffs, N.J.: Prentice-Hall, 1958.

Richmond, Douglas W., ed. *Essays on the Mexican War.* College Station: Texas A&M University Press, 1986.

Ripley, Roswell S. *The War with Mexico.* 2 vols. New York: Harper and Bros., 1849.

Roa Bárcena, José María. *Recuerdos de la invasión norteamericana (1846–1848).* Mexico: J. Buxó y Cía., 1883.

Robinson, Cecil, ed. *The View from Chapultepec: Mexican Writers on the Mexican-American War.* Tucson: University of Arizona Press, 1989.

Sandweiss, Martha A., Rick Stewart, and Ben W. Huseman. *Eyewitness to War: Prints and Daguerrotypes of the Mexican War, 1846–1848.* Ft. Worth, Tex.: Amon Carter Museum; Washington, D.C.: Smithsonian Institution Press, 1989.

Santa Anna, Antonio López de. *The Eagle: The Autobiography of Santa Anna.* Ed. Ann Fears Crawford. Austin, Tex.: Pemberton Press, 1967.

Schlicke, Carl P. *General George Wright: Guardian of the Pacific Coast.* Norman: University of Oklahoma Press, 1988.

Sears, Louis M. *John Slidell.* Durham: Duke University Press, 1925. S.v. "Slidell's Mission to Mexico," ch. 5.

Sellers, Charles. *James K. Polk, Continentalist, 1843–1846.* Princeton, N.J.: Princeton University Press, 1966.

Singletary, Otis A. *The Mexican War.* Chicago, Ill.: University of Chicago Press, 1960.

Smith, Ephraim Kirby. *To Mexico with Scott; The Letters of Captain E. Kirby Smith to his Wife.* Ed. Emma Jerome Blackwood. Cambridge, Mass.: Harvard University Press, 1917.

Smith, George W., and Charles Judah, eds. *Chronicles of the Gringos: The U.S. Army in the Mexican War, 1846–1848; Accounts of Eyewitnesses and Combatants.* Albuquerque: University of New Mexico Press, 1968.

Smith, Justin H. *The War with Mexico.* 2 vols. New York: Macmillan, 1919.

Spiller, Roger J., ed. *Dictionary of American Military Biography.* 3 vols. Westport, Conn.: Greenwood Press, 1984.

Stenberg, Richard R. "The Failure of Polk's Mexican War Intrigues of 1845," *The Pacific Historical Review* 4 (Mar., 1935): 35–68.

Toussaint, Manuel. *La catedral y las iglesias de Puebla.* Mexico: Editorial Porrúa, 1954.

Tutorow, Norman E. *The Mexican-American War: An Annotated Bibliography.* Westport, Conn.: Greenwood Press, 1981.

United States. Congress. Senate. "Message from the President, Dec. 7, 1847." *Senate Exec. Doc. No. 1,* 30th Cong., 1st Sess., 1847.

Vásquez, Josefina Z., and Lorenzo Meyer. *The United States and Mexico.* Chicago, Ill.: University of Chicago Press, 1985.

"A Visit to Popocatepetl," *Putnam's Monthly Magazine* 1 (Apr., 1853): 408–16.

Wallace, Edward S. *General William Jenkins Worth: Monterrey's Forgotten Hero.* Dallas, Tex.: Southern Methodist University Press, 1953.

Weems, John Edward. *To Conquer a Peace: The War Between the United States and Mexico.* College Station: Texas A&M University Press, 1988.

Weigley, Russell F. *History of the United States Army.* New York: Macmillan, 1967.

Wilcox, Cadmus M. *History of the Mexican War.* Ed. Mary R. Wilcox. Washington, D.C.: Church News Publishing Co., 1892.

Index

The Mexican War Journal and Letters of Ralph W. Kirkham was composed into type on a Compugraphic digital phototypesetter in eleven point Baskerville with two points of spacing between the lines. Baskerville was also selected for display. The book was designed by Jim Billingsley, typeset by Metricomp, Inc., printed offset by Thomson-Shore, Inc., and bound by John H. Dekker & Sons, Inc. The paper on which this book is printed carries acid-free characteristics for an effective life of at least three hundred years.

Texas A&M University Press : College Station